D0088871

Advance Praise for *The Death of Politics*

"At a moment when our parties are broken and Washington divided and angry, Wehner offers ways Americans can have a more civil, productive political conversation. Agree with his prescriptions or not, the reader will finish this book having met a man of faith, integrity, and patriotism."

—Karl Rove, former senior advisor and deputy chief of staff for President George W. Bush

"In an era of craven capitulation by so-called Christian leaders, Peter Wehner is one of the few public evangelicals who has been a persistent critic of Trump. In this important book, Wehner not only reminds us of the virtues necessary to sustain the American experiment, he also offers a timely apologetic for politics as a profession and a calling. I hope this book finds its way into the hands of a younger generation who has yet to see what healthy political deliberation looks like."

—James K. A. Smith, author of *You Are What You Love*

"Wehner makes a powerful case that politics is a noble calling that has been corrupted by Donald Trump. An important book."

—John C. Danforth, former Republican US senator from Missouri

"Highly recommended for all who care about the restoration of civility to American politics."

—Gary Hart, former Democratic US senator from Colorado

"A seasoned political realist and a humble Christian disciple, Wehner clarifies, reminds, rehearses, enjoins, and inspires us to take up our citizenship anew."

—Mark Labberton, president of Fuller Theological Seminary

"With unflinching honesty and sincere hope, Wehner examines how the body politic of America has fallen so low and how it might regain its place as the hope of the world."

—Bishop Claude Alexander, The Park Church

"Thoughtful, incisive, and provocative, Peter Wehner's meditation on where we are—and where we must go—is essential and timely reading. Conservatives need it, but so do all Americans, because whether we like it or not, we are all in this search for a more perfect union together."

—Jon Meacham, author of *The Soul of America*

"As the son of German immigrants, Wehner understands the cataclysmic impact of countries that get politics wrong. In these grim political times, this is a book of hope."

—Joe Scarborough, host of *Morning Joe*

"A conservative's reasoned indictment of President Trump, a moving appeal for public truth-telling, and practical strategies for combining civility with conviction."

—Mark Noll, author of *The Scandal of the Evangelical Mind*

"Like a literary Paul Revere, Wehner raises his lantern in this urgent work, shining a light on the causes of the withering polarization that has seized our democracy and reminds each of us what we must do to save it."

—David Axelrod, director of the University of Chicago Institute of Politics and CNN senior political commentator

"Learned, humane, and wise, Wehner's worried, yet not despairing, guidance comes just when it is most needed."

—Mona Charen, author of *Sex Matters* and *Useful Idiots*

The
DEATH
of
POLITICS

How to Heal Our Frayed
Republic After Trump

PETER WEHNER

HarperOne
An Imprint of HarperCollinsPublishers

HarperOne

HarperCollins books may be purchased for educational, business, or sales promotional use. For information, please email the Special Markets Department at SPsales@harpercollins.com.

FIRST EDITION

Designed by Michelle Crowe

Library of Congress Cataloging-in-Publication Data has been applied for.

ISBN 978-0-06-282079-2

19 20 21 22 23 LSC 10 9 8 7 6 5 4 3 2 1

To my parents, who nurtured my love for politics and
my love for America

Contents

CHAPTER 1

A Noble Calling

This is a book that pushes back against what people have come to think about *politics*. The word itself conjures in our minds an image that is nasty, brutish, and depressing. My aim, however, is to leave you far more hopeful about politics than you are, because you have far more power than you think.

Even I need to be reminded of this, as someone who has spent my whole career in politics, where I've seen the good, the bad, and the ugly; where things work and things fail; and where I've encountered men and women of integrity, as well as scoundrels. I've worked as a college intern in the Washington State legislature, as a senior advisor in the White House, and in the previous three Republican administrations. Today, in my current capacity as a *New York Times* contributing opinion writer, contributing writer for *The Atlantic*, and frequent commentator on political talk shows, my focus has been on the general calamity caused by President Trump.

In such a context it's not always easy to get beyond fear and worry, deep disappointment, and a sense of genuine outrage at what is being done to the profession I value and the nation I love.

This book, then, has been beneficial for me; I hope it will be for you as well. We have lost sight of who we are as a people and as a nation. We need to relearn what American politics ought to be about, and we need to realize that as citizens we have the power and ability to repair the fraying we have witnessed.

Here's the problem: when Americans think about politics today, their first thought is that it is inherently dirty and undignified; that most politicians are corrupt and unprincipled, either knaves or fools; that those involved in politics only care about their self-interest and not at all about the interest of the country; that it takes no special skills to be a politician—in fact the less experience, the better; that the problems we face as a nation are simple, the solutions obvious, so either stupidity or malice must explain why the solutions haven't been implemented yet.

Many people today have given up on politics, believing it to be irredeemable, and their frustrations are understandable.

We are indeed at a low ebb in the history of modern American politics—a period when politics is both trivial and dehumanizing, when large challenges are being either ignored or made worse, and when politics is an arena for invective. Virtually across the board, in both parties, the political leadership ranges from mediocre to dismal. Republicans and Democrats have contempt for each other. They can't work together to solve our common problems. And the most important and powerful political office in the world is occupied by a man who is intellectually, temperamentally, and morally unfit to be mayor of a small city, let alone president of the United States.

"It's just messed up now" is how one woman put it to the *Washington Post*. "It's not even a political system. It's a reality show."

Another said American democracy has become "a rock-throwing contest."[1]

But that is not the whole story. To hold a uniformly negative view of politics is selective and misleading—and in important ways it is simply wrong. It mistakenly assumes that our current predicament is a permanent condition. But just as a television series shouldn't be judged by a single bad episode, just as a professional basketball player shouldn't be judged by a single bad series, politics shouldn't be judged by its worst moments. Certainly American politics has seen moments of squalor, but our politics has also seen moments of grandeur. Most of the time it's something in between. Here is the risk of allowing ourselves to be cynical: When we imagine that this nadir is the norm, we let ourselves and our leaders off the hook. We imply that there is no point in demanding better or in working to do better.

In fact, it is precisely at a low point like this one that we should remind ourselves of the potential of politics, both to better understand what has gone wrong and to think more concretely about how to turn our politics around. We simply cannot afford to settle for the reigning arguments that politics is beyond repair and our corrupt leaders and institutions are to blame. The core argument of this book is altogether different. It will argue that by remembering and restoring America's noble and necessary political tradition—covering the roles of morality, religion, rhetoric, debate, and citizenship—we can heal what has been fractured and get back to the task of making America a more perfect union.

Much of the blame for our ugly and unfortunate state of affairs can be laid at the feet of politicians and the political class, of which I have been very much a part. Not everyone is culpable, of course, but as a general matter our elites have been detached from the problems and creeping hopelessness that have overwhelmed many Americans, especially those without college degrees and those who are living in rural areas.

Rather than shaping events, Republican and Democratic lawmakers have often seemed at the mercy of them. The last several years have been characterized by unusual pessimism, a deep sense of unease and apprehension. We've witnessed a collapse of trust in government, particularly the federal government; and that loss of trust is in important ways justified.

But "we the people" are complicit in this state of affairs, too. In a self-governing nation, we generally get the government we deserve. The people who serve in public office haven't been installed by some hostile alien force. It's ordinary Americans—in congressional districts, in states, and in the nation as a whole—who elect House members, senators, governors, and presidents.

Your reaction to politicians as a class may be "To hell with them"—but "To hell with *them*" really means "To hell with *us*." It's just too easy for all of us—myself included—to point the finger at others and never at ourselves, to assume that the troubles plaguing American politics have everything to do with other people and nothing to do with me. We quickly and mercilessly condemn what we consider to be a very unattractive garden (politics) without giving a moment's thought to the role of those tasked with planting the garden's flowers (voters).

The rancor and division in our politics reflect the rancor and division in our nation. It's too facile to say we have a healthy country but a broken political system; in fact, our broken political system reflects the brokenness of our country.

But here is the most important point you should take away

from this book: *what's broken can be mended*. We are not in the grip of forces we can't control. We can reverse what has gone wrong; we can build on what has gone right.

The wrong way to think about politics today is as if we're collectively afflicted by a terminal disease, an illness with no cure. The better way to think about politics is that we're out of shape, the result of doing a lot of things wrong over the years. Shedding pounds and rebuilding muscle is difficult, but it can be done and we know how to do it. It's a matter of summoning the requisite will, energy, and commitment.

So the task before us isn't easy, but it's hardly beyond us. If we demand more of our politicians by demanding more of ourselves, our politics will get better—and so will our country. But that requires us, person by person, to assume the mantle of citizenship.

ESCAPING THE SLOUGH OF DESPOND

I have spent my entire adult life involved in politics in one way or another. I served in the Reagan and George H. W. Bush administrations and, for seven years, in the George W. Bush White House, where I was deputy director of speechwriting before becoming the director of the Office of Strategic Initiatives, a kind of in-house White House think tank. I have been involved in two presidential campaigns, in 2004 (George W. Bush's reelection) and 2012 (Mitt Romney's), and have worked in several leading public policy and research institutions.

All told, then, I have more than three and a half decades in political and public life—in and out of government, formulating and implementing policy, writing speeches for those holding high public office and writing columns and essays about them. I have been a commentator on events and at the center of events, including during the terrorist attacks against America on September 11, 2001. I have seen how politics works up close, including in the West Wing and the Oval Office, and at more of a distance, as a writer and essayist.

But my perspective was also shaped by my early years. Politics was, along with sports, one of my early passions. Among my fondest memories is as a young boy driving with my parents to our cabin in the Cascade Mountains in Washington State in the 1970s and talking about current events—at that time, the end of the Vietnam War and the 1973 Mideast war, Henry Kissinger's shuttle diplomacy and Richard Nixon's opening to China, the Watergate hearings and the Nixon pardon, and the Carter-Ford election among them. I became an avid reader of books, magazines, and the newspaper. My parents and I would watch the evening news together and discuss what we saw. And some of my most vivid recollections from junior high and high school are of debating my social studies teachers about political and world events.

I never ran for office, not even for student government, and I never had much of a desire to do so. Part of it, I'm sure, was a fear of failure and not wanting to be the focus of attention. I was also afraid of public speaking, something that took me years to overcome. But what most drew me to politics were the ideas and personalities, the human drama, the ability to shape events and outcomes, the sense that there was something important and meaningful at stake. Both my parents immigrated to America from Germany, so I understood from an early age the cataclysm that can follow when we get politics wrong.

I pursued a life in politics in part out of a sense of its high possibilities, then, and most other people in politics chose that path for similar reasons. This is one important reason for my sense that our politics is not only salvageable but a potential source of renewal and recovery for the country. The political arena is actually full of people who love their country and want to serve it. They are also, of course, ambitious, driven, and eager to advance. Right now, the incentives that too often confront them in politics put their ideals in tension with their personal ambitions. But it need not be that way, and part of what a revival of our politics would involve is a better alignment of the incentives our politicians face with the potential of politics to elevate our national life. That, too, is why only a change of attitude among the broader public could bring about such a revival. Citizens who demand more will yield politicians who offer more. I know this can work because I have seen it work.

All in all, it has been a fascinating journey. I'm hardly naive about politics—about the capacity of power to dull the conscience of good people, about the degraded state of our discourse, about how political loyalty and partisanship can cause people who should know better to act in maddeningly hypocritical ways. Politics is a fallen profession composed of fallen people. But of course that is true of the medical and legal professions, of real estate agencies and the academy, of churches and auto repair shops, of hedge fund managers and waiters, janitors and store clerks, radio talk show hosts and mathematicians, actors and athletes. My inner Christian, as well as my inner realist, starts out by acknowledging the fallenness of all humanity.

Today too many people seem determined to see politics in part rather than in whole. They focus on the downside while ignoring the upside, in a way that's unbalanced, unrealistic, and therefore untrue. I understand the temper of our times, and I know it's fashionable to be cynical. But I intend to help readers see that those who are cynical about politics are the ones who are actually naive.

I would be delighted if you took away from this book a sense that politics is not only a necessary activity but a noble calling—an imperfect but essential way to advance justice and human flourishing. This may seem unimaginable during our angry and distrustful time, when so much of politics seems both trivial and malicious. But it happens to be true.

In his classic seventeenth-century allegory *Pilgrim's Progress*, John Bunyan describes the protagonist, Christian, who has heedlessly fallen into the Slough of Despond, where he "wallowed for a time, being grievously bedaubed with the dirt; and . . . began to sink in the mire." But along comes a figure, Help, who "gave [Christian] his hand, and he drew him out; and set him upon some ground, and bade him go on his way."

We've been wallowing for too long in a political Slough of Despond, bedaubed with the dirt, sunk in the mire. This book is a modest attempt to help draw us out, to once again set us on firm ground, and to get us back on our way.

CHAPTER 2

How We Ended Up
in This Mess

O n January 14, 2016—half a year after Donald Trump descended an escalator at Trump Tower to announce his run for the presidency and several months before he wrapped up the Republican presidential nomination—I wrote a column in the *New York Times* in which I declared I would not vote for him under any circumstances.

I was perhaps the first prominent Republican to have taken this position, and I did so despite having voted Republican in every presidential election since I first became eligible to vote in 1980, despite having worked in three Republican administrations, and despite having worked for Republican presidential campaigns.

"Party loyalty has limits," I wrote.

In this case, the limits were rooted in my belief that Mr. Trump was intellectually, psychologically, and temperamentally unfit to be president. I argued that Trump is precisely the kind of person our system of government was designed to avoid, the type of demagogic leader our founders feared.

I also warned that Trump posed a profound threat to the Republican Party and conservatism, in ways that Hillary Clinton never could. Mrs. Clinton could inflict a defeat on the Republican Party, but she could not redefine it. Mr. Trump, if he were to win, could redefine it from a conservative party to an angry, bigoted, populist one.

My stance was dramatically out of step with that of many of my friends and acquaintances, most of whom are Republicans. I had countless conversations with Trump supporters—some enthusiastic, others more qualified—who expressed their unhappiness with my views. How could I not cast a vote for the GOP nominee in a race against *Hillary Clinton*, of all people?

In the course of those discussions—almost all of them reasonably civil, if sometimes fairly intense—several themes emerged. One of the most frequent ones was the idea that the country was on the brink of collapse and that we needed someone to shake the system to its foundation. A person I have known for many years wrote me during the Republican primaries. What he said is typical of what I heard:

I think we have likely slipped past the point of no return as a country and I'm desperately hoping for a leader who can turn us around. I have no hope that one of the establishment guys would do that. That, I believe, is what opens people up to Trump. He's all the bad things you say, but what has the Republican establishment given me in the past 16 years? First and foremost: BHO [a derogatory acronym for Barack Obama by his critics, meant to highlight his middle name, Hussein].

What's notable in this exchange is that the person who sent it to me didn't deny Trump's drawbacks, but they hardly seemed to matter. For many Trump supporters, things couldn't possibly get worse, so electing Trump was worth a roll of the dice. The supposition was that he's really no worse than many other politicians, and in some respects he's better than they are.

Desperate times require desperate actions, and these are desperate times. Or so the story goes. But is the story actually true?

THE POLITICS OF CONTEMPT

This book began to take shape, for me, from the realization that any nation that elects Donald Trump to be its president has a dangerously low view of politics.

This statement isn't simply a supposition; it points to a serious problem. Donald Trump is the culmination of a long-term destructive trend: the public's utter contempt for politics. By *contempt* I don't mean merely extreme frustration or anger over what is happening politically. Such reactions have been apparent in America since our first contested election in 1800. Something new is afoot in our political lives. By *contempt*, I am describing how many Americans have crossed over a threshold from frustration to despair, from unhappiness to rage, from deep skepticism to corrosive cynicism. Many Americans have lost hope that we can solve our problems using the traditional means of politics. This is a very dangerous development; it opens us up to all sorts of anticonstitutional mischief.

What is the result of this contempt? At a time when it's imperative for Americans to recover a sense of the high purposes of politics, they elected as president a man who seems determined to denigrate it. Trump in this sense is a symptom at least as much as a cause of the virus now threatening our common life in America. There is a very real sense that Trump's presidency could mark the death of the best of the American tradition of politics. If this happens, it would be a catastrophic loss.

One of the duties we have as citizens, regardless of our political affiliations, is to look searchingly and honestly at the nature of this virus—what caused it, what sustains it, and what needs to be done to combat it and ameliorate its effects. And that is what I want to undertake here. To start, and it is only a start, let's examine Trump's rise and what it says about the state of American politics.

Donald Trump ran for president in 2016 with no experience and no obvious qualifications for the job. Over the course of nearly a dozen presidential primary debates and countless interviews, speeches, and Twitter storms, Trump showed he was unsuited to be president. The former reality television show star proved himself to be a huckster and a con man, a peddler of conspiracy theories and a compulsive liar, vindictive and erratic, and staggeringly ignorant of the key political issues of the day. Often his answers amounted to a word salad—a confused mixture of seemingly random and repetitive phrases. I don't make these claims out of political rancor; all of them are reasonable verdicts based on cold, hard facts.

What was alarming, though, was that none of this seemed to matter—and weirdly, some of it seemed to help him.

To many Trump voters, he was an agent of change, a "street fighter" who hits back against his critics many times harder than they hit him, a man who was "authentic" and not "politically correct." To his core supporters Trump was a wrecking ball against the much-loathed "establishment," or a man who would "drain the swamp." His inexperience and sheer abnormality were seen as marks in his favor. He wasn't part of the problem. He was an outsider—in his case, it was said, a successful businessman and deal maker—in a nation that perceived politics as broken.

How broken? A Washington Post–University of Maryland poll in 2017, the year Trump assumed office, revealed "a starkly pessimistic view of U.S. politics, widespread distrust of the nation's political leaders and their ability to compromise, and an erosion of pride in the way democracy works in America."[1]

Among the findings was that just 14 percent of Americans said they view the ethics and honesty of politicians as excellent or good. Seven in ten Americans said the nation's politics have reached a dangerous low point, and a majority of those believe the situation is a "new normal" rather than temporary. The same number, seven in ten, said the nation's political divisions are at least as deep as during the Vietnam War.

A Gallup poll the following year, 2018, found that fewer than half of those surveyed, 47 percent, said they are "extremely proud" to be an American, a record low. Fifteen years earlier the figure was 70 percent.[2]

"I'm old enough that I remember the Vietnam War," Ed Evans, a sixty-seven-year-old lawyer in Sioux Falls, South Dakota, said in an interview with the *Post*. "With Vietnam, at least it was focused on one issue. Here, it's all over the place. In some ways, this is deeply more troubling."

"This country is a mess" is how Ellen Collins, an independent who is a retired data architect in Dayton, Ohio, put it. "There's no civility. Friends are now enemies. These issues have made people angry."[3]

Mutual contempt between Republicans and Democrats is rapidly rising, and sizable shares of both Democrats and Republicans say the other party stirs feelings of not just frustration but fear and anger.[4]

I've experienced this firsthand, as former colleagues as well as even close friends and relatives have not simply criticized my views of President Trump but argued that my anti-Trump stance is a product of seeking fortune and fame among the liberal intelligentsia. My politics wasn't simply wrong, in other words; it was a manifestation of a character flaw.

"I can appreciate the reasons you possibly sold out to the D.C. cartel, Pete (survival and keeping groceries on the table are powerful motivators), but it still pains me to realize that someone I have admired for so long did so," a distant relative I have always gotten along with wrote to me in 2017. "Why did you decide that you had to go with the prevailing winds in D.C. to preserve a career?"

At the same time, public trust in the government is near historic lows. Three-quarters of Americans believe it is a serious problem that the political system in Washington is not working well enough to produce solutions to the nation's problems.[5]

So how did we get to this moment?

The answer is complicated, and as with any broad trend there are many contributing and converging factors. But four are worth emphasizing because they go a long way toward helping us understand where we are: (1) massive demographic and cultural changes, which many see as redefining what it means to be American; (2) long-term income stagnation for most workers, which provokes middle-class economic anxieties; (3) the ongoing polarization of our political parties at the cost of not solving America's problems; and (4) the resulting loss of trust in the political class.

Let's briefly explore each of them in order.

DEMOGRAPHIC DISRUPTION

The conventional analysis in the aftermath of Donald Trump's improbable victory in 2016 is that it was primarily the result of economic anxieties among blue-collar, working-class whites. But recent studies indicate that something else, something more visceral, was also going on.

Many Trump voters—mostly male, white, and Christian— were driven by cultural anxiety, a fear of losing their status in society, and a longing to regain a sense of social dominance.

"It's much more of a symbolic threat that people feel," Diana C. Mutz, the author of the study and a political science and communications professor at the University of Pennsylvania, told the *New York Times*. "It's not a threat to their own economic well-being; it's a threat to their group's dominance in our country over all."[6]

Her study challenged the claim that economic anxiety was the main reason people voted for Trump, finding instead that social displacement played a large role. "It used to be a pretty good deal to be a white, Christian male in America, but things have changed and I think they do feel threatened," Dr. Mutz said. She told the *Times* that Trump support was linked to a belief that high-status groups, such as whites, Christians, or men, faced more discrimination than low-status groups, like minorities, Muslims, or women.

Another study, this one a survey by the Public Religion

Research Institute and *The Atlantic*, found that "fears about immigrants and cultural displacement were more powerful factors than economic concerns in predicting support for Trump among white working-class voters."[7]

The data on white working-class Americans are striking: nearly two-thirds of white working-class Americans believe America's culture and way of life have deteriorated since the 1950s; nearly half say that "things have changed so much that I often feel like a stranger in my own country"; nearly seven in ten believe the American way of life needs to be protected from foreign influence; and nearly seven in ten white working-class Americans believe the US is in danger of losing its culture and identity.

The scale of these shifts is enormous. Earlier in this decade, and for the first time in American history, people who say they are "white" and "Christian" constituted less than 50 percent of the population in America. White Christians are now a minority. Students of color now make up a majority of public school pupils. Almost 40 percent of the population is nonwhite, double what it was in 1980. Meanwhile, the foreign-born population in the United States—13.7 percent of the total population—has reached its highest share since 1910. (In 1970, the foreign-born population was less than 5 percent.)[8]

We've seen equally dramatic changes in the arenas of culture, family, and human sexuality. The share of American adults who have never married is at an all-time high. Half of adults are married today, compared to 72 percent in 1960.[9] Two-parent households are in decline (from 88 percent in 1960 to 69 percent today),[10] and 40 percent of all births are to unwed mothers.[11] Nearly half of two-parent households have a mother and father who both work.[12] Gay marriage, which not that many years ago was considered unthinkable, is today the law of the land and has widespread public support. That issue is now settled in the minds of most Americans; the next boundary has to do with transgender rights.

For many Americans, these changes have been deeply unsettling.

To focus on a subgroup with which I am quite familiar: in the span of a generation, evangelical Christians have gone from seeing themselves as a "moral majority" to an embattled minority. I have talked to evangelical authors, academics, college presidents, and nonprofit leaders about this; they describe reactions among Christians ranging from angry combativeness to disillusioned withdrawal.

John Inazu, the author of *Confident Pluralism: Surviving and Thriving Through Deep Difference*, told me he has seen in some circles "an insecurity caused by a rapidly lost social position," leading some to a "growing bitterness and despair."[13]

A consequence of all of this is that the factions of our politics, the subgroups contending for their separate causes, have all become more philosophically and culturally uniform, widening the differences between groups and making it nearly impossible to find common ground. Essentially what is happening is that those who are comfortable with demographic and cultural changes are identifying as Democrats while those who are uncomfortable with those changes are identifying as Republicans—and never the twain shall meet.[14]

And this is important to recognize: these differences are over issues that many people are particularly impassioned about. They are fundamental differences over the deepest questions. The result is that our politics is inflamed. Those on the right view their opponents as intent on destroying America as they conceive of it; those on the left view their opponents as benighted, bigoted, and cruel.

It's an explosive mix.

ECONOMIC ANXIETIES AND THE MIDDLE CLASS

Changes in demography provide only one piece of the puzzle, however. Economics is another.

As I write this, America is experiencing quite a long period of growth—we're closing in on the longest economic expansion in modern US history—combined with low unemployment, low inflation, and low interest rates. Confidence in the economy is rising a decade after a savage recession. A 2018 report issued by the Federal Reserve Board found that nearly three-quarters of adults said they were either doing okay or living comfortably, over 10 percentage points more than in the first survey in 2013.[15]

At the same time, growth in both GDP (gross domestic product) and wages has been low by historical standards. Real GDP growth in the twenty-first century has been significantly below what it was during the latter half of the twentieth century,[16] while over the course of the past two decades, under both Republican and Democratic rule, median household income has been essentially flat. This stagnation, lasting over the course of an entire generation, is without parallel in postwar America.[17] Many Americans feel as if they've been either spinning their wheels or sliding backward.

The political commentator Ron Brownstein, in analyzing data about the attitudes of Americans spanning the years just prior to the 2016 election, concluded, "The overall message is of pervasive, entrenched vulnerability—a sense that many financial milestones once assumed as cornerstones of middle-class life are now beyond reach for all but the rich."[18]

That anxious mood of Americans, very much including the American middle class, is not simply a problem of morale. It has been rooted, at least in part, in real circumstances and actual struggles.

Since 2000, the middle class has shrunk in size and fallen backward in income and wealth. For most American workers, real wages—that is, after inflation is taken into account—have been flat or even falling for decades, regardless of whether the economy was adding or subtracting jobs.

At the same time, we've seen health-care costs skyrocket while the cost of going to college has consistently risen faster than inflation.[19] Middle-class Americans are working longer hours than they did in the late 1970s—on average more than two hundred more hours per year—even as they're losing ground.

To the extent that the economy has been growing, its blessings have been asymmetrical, with real-wage growth (excluding benefits, largely health benefits) being zero or negative for the bottom 80 percent of the population since 2008, while about 85 percent of the stock market gains have flowed to the top 10 percent of the population.[20] This has exacerbated income inequality, which began to rise in the late 1970s and has generally continued to widen under both Democratic and Republican presidents.

Meanwhile, the chances of moving up and down the income ladder are basically what they've been for decades—which is to say, they are very low. Today a child's future depends on parental income more in America than it does in Canada or Europe. And the odds of escaping poverty are about half as high in the United States as in more mobile countries like Denmark.[21]

We shouldn't underestimate the effects of immobility on our national psyche. Social mobility, after all, is central to how people in the United States interpret the America Dream. It has always been part of our self-conception, our self-understanding, and it's being stripped away.

Complicating matters still further is that we are living through a period of enormous economic transformation and disruption, caused in part by huge advances in technology and automation of production. This allows businesses to do more with less, thus making greater and greater profits with fewer and fewer workers.

It's often said that the American manufacturing sector is in decline, but in fact manufacturing is declining in terms of *employment*, not in terms of *output* or its share of the economy. The increasing efficiency of American manufacturing has come at the expense of lower-skilled workers. Jobs, including even higher-skilled jobs, are being outsourced to countries like China and India as the economy grows more globalized. Arguably the increased labor-market competition resulting from recent mass immigration puts downward pressure on wages for Americans with lower levels of education and skills, even as it reduces the cost of living for Americans higher up the income distribution.

So what does all of this have to do with the frustration and anger aimed at politicians? The answer is simple, probably too simple: a majority of middle-class adults put most of the blame squarely on the government for the economic difficulties they have faced, and people blame Congress more than any other institution.[22]

I say "too simple" because we have experienced historic shifts in the global economy over the last several decades that politicians did not cause and were often powerless to stop. The entrance of China and other Asian nations into the global economy brought more than a billion low-wage workers into direct competition with American workers in this century. There are intrinsic limitations on what politicians can (and should) do to stop globalization, automation, and advances in technology. The horse-and-buggy industry gave way to the automobile industry, which was a disruptive but unquestionably positive change.

We live in an increasingly high-skill economy, which means opportunities for lower-skill workers are dwindling. This requires political responses and government action that have not been forthcoming, but the changes themselves are not the *fault* of government.

For now, though, many Americans remain anxious and unnerved, worried about the long-term trajectory of the economy, and they believe the political and governing class has let them down.

POLARIZATION, DISTRUST, INVECTIVE

Moving from the realm of immense cultural change and long-term economic anxiety to the actual practice of politics, we find dysfunction rooted in polarization, the result of the Republican and Democratic Parties having become "more internally homogeneous and more ideologically distant from each other."[23] Many Americans are rightly upset because politics has become an arena for intensely heated and largely unproductive conflict. (If the conflict was heated but productive, it would at least be tolerable.)

Politics should be informed by principles and ideals and by a vision of the human good and the nature of society, but it must also answer to real needs and concerns. Many people feel, and with plenty of justification, that that's not happening right now. They believe politics has become first and foremost an arena for insults, for abuse, for pettiness.

The long-term trends already discussed—ones that predate Donald Trump's entry into politics but have been amplified by him—have brought us to this moment.

Today the two parties are ideologically purer, and farther apart, than at any time since the Reconstruction period following the Civil War, according to Professors Jonathan Haidt and Sam Abrams. Liberal Republicans and conservative Democrats are nearly extinct. But what's most notable is that Americans have also begun to sort themselves not just politically, but also in terms of lifestyle choices and interests, by geography and faith. We increasingly live in separate worlds, interacting less often, understanding one another less well.

The transformation of media has accelerated the silo-ization of America. There are now hundreds of partisan news sources— including cable news, blogs, the internet, and social media—we can turn to in order to convince ourselves that we're right and righteous and the other side is not only wrong but criminal or evil.

"This proliferation of sources interacts with our most notorious problem in human cognition: the confirmation bias," according to Haidt and Abrams.[24] We seek out evidence to confirm what we already believe.

For his part, the journalist Jonathan Rauch argues that our severely fractured political system is plagued with a "chaos syndrome." For decades we've demonized and disempowered political professionals and parties, he argues, leaving the system vulnerable to disorder and upheaval, with the current state of affairs just the latest symptom. As the influence of the "intermediaries" fades, he writes, "politicians, activists, and voters all become more individualistic and unaccountable. The system atomizes. Chaos becomes the new normal—both in campaigns and in the government itself."[25]

In other words, ideological purification has given rise to political polarization, which in turn has led to an intensification in the animosity people of different parties have for one another. The result is gridlock and dysfunction, which has naturally instilled increasing frustration and impatience with the system as a whole. And the result of that is a greater willingness, even an eagerness, to embrace political leaders who will break the usual rules and shatter the usual restraints to get things done.

CONTEMPT FOR THE POLITICAL CLASS

A fourth explanation for the degraded state of American politics, which follows from the first three, has to do with the practical failures of politicians and the political elite, individuals who are office holders and their staffs, those who comment on politics and who design and implement public policy.

The indictment against the establishment includes a detachment from and an indifference toward the hardships facing tens of millions of Americans over the last several years: lost jobs; people dropping out of the labor force; stagnant wages; lack of upward mobility; rising hopelessness and addiction; growing income inequality; soaring health-care costs; failing schools, particularly in our rural communities and urban centers; and an erosion of family and community life.

Some of that disconnection is the result of callousness, but much more of it is the result of cultural separation and living in a world that is walled off from many of the hardships facing working-class Americans.

The social scientist Charles Murray refers to the "SuperZIPS," zip codes that are home to the hyperwealthy and hyperelite. He reports that if you rank all the zip codes in the country on an index of education and income and group them by percentiles, you will find that eleven of thirteen Washington, DC–area zip codes are in the ninety-ninth percentile and the other two in the ninety-eighth. Ten of them are in the top half of the ninety-ninth percentile.[26] Translation: lawmakers and their staffs work and live in some of the most elite, rarified air in America. That world is profoundly different from most of the rest of the country and certainly from those parts of the country that are struggling, vulnerable, and in some cases simply dying away.

To be sure, there has always been an elite in America that was overrepresented in our political institutions, but this tended to happen in eras when public life often brought forward people of exceptional skill and ability. For example, the years immediately following World War II surfaced men like Dean Acheson, President Truman's secretary of state who was the architect of the Truman Doctrine and a proponent of NATO; General George C. Marshall, chief of staff for the army in World War II, secretary of state and defense, and winner of the Nobel Peace Prize in 1953 for his role in promoting the sweeping economic recovery program for Europe; and George Kennan, American diplomat, historian, advocate for the containment of the Soviet Union, and intellectual darling of the Washington establishment. All were men who were reckoned, even by those who disagreed with them, to be extraordinary doers and thinkers.

Perhaps the main difference between the elite then and now is competence. The postwar generation achieved extraordinary successes and built institutions and alliances that helped shape the world for generations. People will accept political leaders being out of touch with their everyday concerns so long as they improve their everyday lives. The old elite frequently did; the current elite, much less so.

I'm not saying the current governing class doesn't have any successes to their credit; they do. Nor am I saying the problems we face today are simple to solve. They're not. We're confronting economic and cultural changes comparable to those that characterized the Industrial Revolution. But the establishment hasn't found effective ways to assist people through these wrenching transitions. It has barely done a thing to address one of the worst public health crises in American history: the opioid epidemic. (It accounted for more than 47,000 deaths in 2017, while the total number of drug overdose deaths in the US exceeded 70,000.)[27] Nor has the governing class reformed and modernized our badly outdated and inefficient institutions—our tax code; our entitlement programs; or our immigration, criminal justice, financial, and education systems.

To compound matters, both major political parties in America are exhausted and devoid of ideas, often speaking as if the very same solutions they offered a generation or more ago would work equally well today. They won't.

It has been said that for Republicans, every day is January 20,

1981, when Ronald Reagan was inaugurated; and for Democrats, every day is January 20, 1965, when Lyndon Johnson was inaugurated. Those were their halcyon days. But they are gone, and they aren't coming back.

Each party is caught in a time warp, in important ways disconnected from the problems of ordinary Americans and so far unable to do much about them. So it's little wonder that confidence in politics has collapsed.

KEEPING PERSPECTIVE

Think of the four factors I've identified—rapid demographic and cultural changes, middle-class economic anxiety, polarization, and the failures of our governing class—as tributaries of a roiling river. We're at the confluence. People are rightfully frustrated that problems are not getting addressed; that the issues provoking stress, fear, and hardship are hotly debated but never resolved or fixed; that the political elites are out of touch with the issues facing most Americans and focus too much on getting reelected at the expense of solving problems. And so it is certainly understandable why the political mood in the country has shifted from long-term frustration and anger to despair and cynicism about the political process.

But I'd ask you to consider another question: What if those responsible for the problems we face today are not only politicians but also the people who elect them?

In a self-governing nation, blame for the failures of our politics, just like praise for its successes, doesn't fall entirely on elected officials. It's all well and good to bash the political establishment, so long as we bear in mind that "average" Americans—pharmacists and high school teachers, accountants and auto mechanics, police officers and pastors living in Birmingham and Seattle, Salt Lake City and San Francisco, New Orleans and Boulder—have played a part in creating this political system. This is part of what it means to live in a democracy.

"We assume we are better people than we seem to be," according to the historian Wilfred McClay, "and we assume that our politics should therefore be an endlessly uplifting pursuit, full of joy and inspiration and self-actualization rather than endless wrangling, head-butting, and petty self-interest."[28]

Don't forget that "ordinary" Americans elected both Ted Cruz and Elizabeth Warren to the Senate and Jim Jordan of the Freedom Caucus and Alexandria Ocasio-Cortez, a democratic socialist, to the House. It's no surprise they clash; and many Americans want them to clash, to confront the opposition, to fight for their values.

Moreover, majorities of partisans have deeply unfavorable views of people in the other party. As William Galston points out in his book *Anti-Pluralism: The Populist Threat to Liberal Democracy*, recent survey data show that members of each party increasingly see the other party as immoral and closed minded, not just misguided but an actual threat.[29]

Our politics is deeply divided because we the people are deeply divided.

But even as we marvel at the challenges we face, we must also be careful about overstating our problems by romanticizing the past. The United States has faced political crises and polarization well beyond what we're experiencing, the most obvious example being a brutal Civil War that claimed 700,000 lives in a nation of just over 30 million (the equivalent of 7 million Americans dying today).

And there have been other periods of turbulence, including the late 1960s, which was marked by widespread race riots and the Vietnam War, by Kent State and the assassinations of Martin Luther King Jr. and Robert Kennedy, by the bloody 1968 Democratic Convention and the trial of the Chicago Seven, by the counterculture revolution and the sexual revolution. The United States experienced more than 2,500 domestic bombings in just eighteen months in 1971 and 1972, almost five a day.[30] And when it comes to political scandals, let's not forget Watergate, which in 1974 brought down a president and, in the process, deeply divided the nation.

As for the rancor in our elections, it has been a feature of American politics for as long as we've been a nation. The first real political campaign in American history, between Thomas Jefferson and John Adams in 1800, is regarded by scholars as among the nastiest campaigns in American history. According to Kerwin Swint, author of *Mudslingers*, "It reached a level of personal animosity that almost tore apart the young republic and has rarely been equaled in two hundred years of presidential politics."[31]

The 1872 election between Ulysses S. Grant and Horace Greeley is a race the *New York Sun* said deteriorated into "a shower of mud." It wasn't much better a dozen years later, during the 1884 race between Grover Cleveland and James Blaine, when Cleveland was accused of fathering a child out of wedlock. This led supporters of Blaine, who was himself something of an ethical mess, to chant what became a national slogan: "Ma, Ma, where's my pa?" (After Cleveland won the election, his supporters answered: "Gone to the White House, ha, ha, ha!") And despite the deep differences between political figures today, they don't settle their differences the way Alexander Hamilton and Aaron Burr did, by duels at ten paces with flintlock pistols. Nor have we seen anything like the bloodshed in 1856 on the floor of the US Senate, where a Southern congressman beat a Northern senator to within an inch of his life—and for his crime was lauded as a hero throughout the South.

THE WAY FORWARD

We shouldn't assume, then, that we're in wholly uncharted territory. The problems we're facing are nowhere near the worst we've faced. And truth be told, politics has been more corrupt in the past than it is today, if only because things are more open and transparent than before.

"I've studied American political corruption throughout the 19th and 20th centuries, and, if anything, corruption was much more common in much of those centuries than today," according to Larry J. Sabato, the director of the University of Virginia's Center for Politics.[32] What has skyrocketed, he argues, is the public *perception* that politicians are corrupt.

That kind of perspective tells us things could be worse. But that doesn't mean our problems are not grave and getting more so. Our political culture is sick. And some of the challenges that characterize this particular moment—the cacophonous, zero-sum nature of our debates; the rampant political tribalism; the fragmentation of the media; the fact that our politics seems to be increasingly trapped in a post-truth world—are worse than I've witnessed in my thirty-five-year career in politics. If they don't change, if we don't first rapidly decelerate and shift course, we may well be involved in a ferocious collision. Today's cycle of recriminations and bitterness, instead of abating, will give way to even greater animosity and spreading violence. That is what I am describing as the death of American politics, when the traditions that have kept us moving forward through past crises have been so undermined that they can no longer function. That is what gives urgency to thinking straight about politics. Because even great countries can decay and hollow out.

This may be the hardest moment, but it is therefore the best time, to be reminded of our past and to make the case that politics is a necessary activity and a moral enterprise. We have a history of many good and able politicians who dedicated themselves to improving people's lives. Yes, politics is part of our problem—but the tradition of American politics can also be part of the solution. The idea that politics will always be as it currently is—that what we're experiencing today is the new and enduring normal, that things can't get better and will only get worse—is a fatalistic trap. We have to avoid it. We must get reacquainted with our history and tradition and find ways to renew and reapply them.

So the task before us, which we will explore in this book, is how we can rediscover, refine, and recalibrate—and in some cases, reenvision and rethink—how we understand politics; to disentangle what politics has become from what it can be, to clear away some of the misconceptions, and to sketch a road map for recovery.

The solution to what ails us lies in large part with changes in attitude, in unlearning some things and in relearning others. We have to reestablish certain fundamentals and be willing to accept that politics is a difficult and sometimes messy business.

"We have now sunk to a depth at which the restatement of the obvious is the first duty of intelligent men," George Orwell said.

Certain things about politics and citizenship that were once obvious no longer are.

Politics is an imperfect profession in an imperfect world. It will never be as good as we want, but it can surely be better than it is. Right now our politics is not equal to the challenges we face. For America to get better, its politics needs to get better. And, yes, for politics to get better, America must get better, too. That's where citizenship comes in.

To be a citizen means to be a participant in civic life, not just a spectator. It means taking the time to be informed and voting in local, state, and national elections. It means seeing the problems America faces for what they are, apportioning in a fair-minded way responsibility for what has gone wrong, and taking ownership of our nation. To be a public-spirited citizen means knowing our history and our stories, the foundations of our political system, and being civically literate.

But that's not all. Responsible citizenship means rewarding leaders who demonstrate integrity and appeal to our better angels rather than our worst impulses, and caring enough about truth to reject propaganda and lies from politicians, pundits, and presidents who spew them.

Being a good citizen means appreciating how our system works, accepting the inherent messiness and difficulty of the process, and engaging the system so that its focus is on solving the problems before us. It also means treating others with whom you have political disagreements as something other than enemies of the state. Being a good citizen means showing some understanding and empathy for those who hold views different than our own, and venturing out of our ideological bubble. And it means becoming a healing agent in our communities and in individual lives.

If our passions are running too high, they can be cooled. If we've become too indifferent to politics at the local and national levels, we can reengage. If we want to learn how those from the past have overcome circumstances more difficult than our own, we can consult history. We can also, in our daily lives, do more to cultivate a sense of gratitude. People who are grateful are more able to dispense grace to others. Gratitude finds ways to express itself; the result is a more humane, decent, and merciful society and political culture.

All of that is easy to say, of course, and harder to do. But it can be done—beginning with understanding the key ideas that have helped shape our politics.

CHAPTER 3

What Politics Is

Before we can repair the state of politics in America, we must first grasp not only what we mean by *politics* but also what is distinctive of its expression in the United States. Contempt for our political practices, even if it is unintentional, denigrates the historical efforts that went into their formation. Much sweat and blood (literally) went into how we developed our traditions; we therefore have a responsibility not to throw away their contributions or our inheritance quite so casually.

My first foray into the nitty-gritty of American politics came early in my career. In 1986, at the tender age of twenty-five, I got an unexpected invitation from the US secretary of education. Bill Bennett, one of the more imposing figures in the conservative movement, wanted me to write speeches for him. I happily agreed. I started at the Department of Education a few months later, and so began my career in government and a close personal relationship with Bennett.

But it was by following him to his next job that I saw more vividly the horror of what can happen when politics fails. During Bennett's tenure as education secretary under President Reagan,

Bennett showed a special interest in the harmful effects of drug use on students, and so it was no surprise that in 1989 he was appointed by the newly elected president, George H. W. Bush, to be the first director of the Office of National Drug Control Policy—or "drug czar," as he was better known. Then, as now, America was facing a drug epidemic.

When President Bush offered him the post of director of the drug policy office, Bennett agreed, and I tagged along with him in the role of special assistant—speechwriter, advisor, traveling companion.

Bennett's tenure didn't last long—less than two years—but during that period he traveled to dozens and dozens of communities, many of them ravaged by drug use. He visited drug treatment facilities, schools in drug-infested neighborhoods, and neonatal intensive care units where "cocaine babies"—born to addicted mothers—struggled to survive. Many of those infants suffered low birth weight, severe and often permanent mental and physical dysfunction or impairment, or signs of drug dependence. Many other such babies—born many weeks or months premature—did not survive past infancy. Experts on child abuse told us time and again that drugs caused a dramatic increase in child abuse and neglect, as crack cocaine turned parents violent and paranoid. Neighborhoods were turned to battle zones.

This was the dark underside of American life, the one most wealthy, upper-middle-class, and middle-class people never saw or wanted to ignore. But life for the less fortunate was sometimes lived in conditions reminiscent of what the seventeenth-century English philosopher Thomas Hobbes called a "state of nature"— the "natural condition of mankind" that would exist if there were no government, no laws, no order. In Hobbes's state of nature, life is "solitary, nasty, brutish and short."

From this I not only learned about the complexity and real suffering behind the problems making their way into our headlines, but I also witnessed something else: what life is like when society breaks down and politics fails, even in a nation as rich and stable as America. Drug epidemics are not fundamentally a function of bad public policy or poor decisions by politicians, yet their emergence and the damage they cause pose challenges that only a society with a functional politics can hope to address. Like many of our society's deepest troubles, they offer reminders of why politics matters.

If we do not step up and repair our politics, the results will damage us more than we can imagine.

THE LONG JOURNEY OF POLITICS

So let's begin by defining what we mean by *politics*. To the ancient Greeks, the term meant "the affairs of the city." Today we understand it to refer to the activities associated with governing, including the debates and conflicts among individuals or parties battling for power. Politics can mean choosing our politicians and running our government, but it can also denote bigger, more fundamental choices about what kind of government (and therefore what kind of society) we will have.

Politics is also about more than policy and problem solving, essential though these are to answering real human needs and concerns. Politics is how we live together and, in a free society like ours, how we ultimately govern ourselves at every level. No successful human society has lived without government, which itself underscores how vital politics is. That was what Aristotle meant when he said, famously, that man is a political animal. Humans have engaged in politics from their first day on this planet.

But our understanding of politics didn't spring out of thin air. Neither is it a static thing, unchanging, frozen in amber. Politics has evolved over time, adjusting to different circumstances, adding and subtracting concepts along the way, sometimes making things better and sometimes worse. We can't know how to heal our politics without understanding a bit of the long journey that has gotten us here.

You will be glad to hear that I will not offer a history of political philosophy since it's well beyond my expertise and beyond the scope of this short book. So what follows is a broad overview of the terrain, essential if blessedly quick.

When I consider the ideas that have shaped and inspired us, three towering figures in particular come to mind: Aristotle, John Locke, and Abraham Lincoln. These are not just individuals from the distant past, the answers to test questions in a high school social studies course, of interest only to historians and biographers. We live in the world they shaped; and every day, knowingly or not, we rely on their insights and discoveries, their words and their works. Articulating their distinctive contributions provides a principled foundation for American politics.

Aristotle

It was Aristotle who won me my first job in government. Sort of. The reason Bill Bennett had heard of me was that I had written an op-ed in the *Washington Times*—sent in over the transom, unsolicited—on what I understood his agenda as secretary of education to be: education should not just be measured by higher test scores and graduation rates but by the goals of education expressed by Aristotle, meaning the cultivation of excellence in human character. This caught Bennett's attention. He called me the morning it was published to express his gratitude.

To suggest that the new secretary of education, who had earned his PhD in political philosophy from the University of Texas, would draw his inspiration from an ancient Greek philosopher was not so odd, really. That's how utterly formative Aristotle's outlook has been for our politics.

Born in 384 BC in northern Greece, Aristotle was a much more systematic thinker and far more empirically and practically minded than his mentor, Plato. (He studied medicine before enrolling in Plato's Academy in his teens, and his scientific cast of mind never left him.) Aristotle was a collector and cataloguer of a huge body of knowledge, deeply curious, a person who prized moderation and warned against extremism and excess.

Over the course of his life, Aristotle showed an amazing mastery of an extraordinary range of subjects, including politics, philosophy, logic, physics and metaphysics, poetry and rhetoric, biology, and psychology. He authored more than two hundred works (most of which have been lost to us), was a tutor of Alexander the Great, and founded his own school at the Lyceum—a friendly rival to Plato's Academy—where he lectured, taught students (often while walking), and wrote his treatises, including most importantly for our purposes, the *Politics*.

Maybe the first thing to understand about the *Politics* is that it was preceded by the *Nicomachean Ethics*, which focused on what it means to live well. The *Ethics* deals with subjects like friendship and contemplation, the pursuit of virtue, pleasure, and human happiness—happiness meaning, for Aristotle, not just joy but human flourishing and deep fulfillment. Aristotle didn't treat ethics and politics as separate categories; instead, he saw the latter as an extension of the former. The connection between the political community and human fulfillment was intimate and essential. For Aristotle, as for many of the ancient Greeks, the proper end of human beings was virtue, good character, and moral excellence, culminating in various kinds of friendship—including that among fellow citizens.

The *Politics*, a classical work of political theory and practice, is an effort to organize and systematize the study of politics—in this case, by examining and classifying the constitutions of 158 states. Aristotle views politics very much as a practical rather than an exclusively theoretical discipline, a means to find unity among people who have different interests. He is wrestling with how the state could function well and how to pursue the common good given the inherent defects in human beings. Aristotle didn't treat politics like a mathematical equation; rather, he understood its complexities and contingencies, which require adjustments and accommodations while holding to core principles and ends. We must, he writes, be content with the precision that is "in accordance with the subject-matter." Answers regarding what is good for particular individuals or states are no more universal and unchanging than answers in the area of medicine.

According to Aristotle, "It is evident that the state is a creation of nature, and that man is by nature a political animal." The polis, or city-state, is not there simply to protect rights or preserve order; its aim is the moral improvement of citizens. Those cities, he says, that merely prevent acts of injustice or facilitate commerce are only cities "in a manner of speaking."[1] Politics should be (and cannot avoid being) deeply involved not simply in policy but in shaping souls. Aristotle time and again refers in his writings to the good life as the chief end of both the community and each of us individually. The state's job includes encouraging goodness and moral improvement. (Aristotle is emphatic about this responsibility, but he is aware of how few states actually do it beyond what is necessary for the regime's stability.)

In the *Nicomachean Ethics*, Aristotle states that the main concern of politics is "to engender a certain character in the citizens and to make them good and disposed to perform noble actions."[2] Ernest Barker, an Aristotle scholar and a translator of the *Politics*, says that to understand how the Greeks viewed the state, we need to think of the church. "Political philosophy thus becomes a sort of moral theology," according to Barker.[3] The polis assumed the tutelary function we tend to ascribe, or once ascribed, to the church.

Aristotle argues that beasts and gods don't need the polis, but humans do—and just as the hand or the foot relies on the rest of the body, we rely on the polis. "Thus the individual needs the city more than the city needs any of its individual citizens," explains Edward Clayton of Central Michigan University.[4]

Greece's supremely great philosophers always had in mind the ideal state, but unlike Plato in his *Republic*, Aristotle was realistic enough to explore the best *attainable* state. "For one should study not only the best regime but also the regime that is [the best] possible, and similarly also the regime that is easier and more attainable for all," he wrote.[5]

Some of Aristotle's views (on women and slavery, for instance) can strike us as primitive and unenlightened; others as downright contemporary and familiar. One of his signal contributions to our modern understanding of politics, for example, is the emphasis he placed on the view that rulers are not above the law, and that leaders should be accountable. We might imagine that he helped set the stage for the rise of constitutional democracies like our own.

But Aristotle held views very different from some key modern thinkers like John Locke, whom we will turn to shortly, when it came to the fundamental relationship between the state and society. The role of politics and government was much more capacious than simply securing the rights and liberties of citizens and providing public safety. The conception of the ancient Greeks, when it came to politics, was that "it encompasses aspects of life which are today regarded as both beyond and beneath politics," according to Carnes Lord, a scholar of Aristotle. "The *Politics* trespasses on ground that would today be claimed by the disciplines of economics, sociology, and urban planning, as well as by moral philosophy and the theory of education."[6] Aristotle goes so far as to discuss the proper age of marriage—eighteen for women and thirty-seven for men—and the proper size of each family.

There's one other area where Aristotle's view of politics is quite different than ours: the seriousness with which the citizens of ancient Greece took their politics. According to the political theorist Alan Ryan:

> No Athenian believed that a Greek could be uninterested in politics. At the very least, self-defense demanded that a man keep a close eye on the holders of power; they understood what Trotsky observed twenty-five hundred years later. "You say you are not interested in politics; but politics is interested in you." The uninterest in politics and the

ignorance about both politicians and political institutions displayed by British or American "citizens" of the present day would have been incomprehensible.[7]

The political scientist Kenneth Minogue said of the ancient Greek: "His very identity was bound up with his city."[8] As we are about to see, while later Western political thinkers built on some of what Aristotle bequeathed them, there was a significant and rather dramatic break with this particular vision of politics, rejecting the view that its highest and most defining purpose was to engage in soulcraft.

The argument that the individual is ultimately best understood as part of the community, or the state, gets some important things right. It emphasizes that no state can be secure without a basis in morality and virtue—and without the support of strong civic education and a vibrant polity. Also, Aristotle was millennia ahead of his time in understanding that human beings cannot be understood merely as freestanding individuals, and that politics is not simply the interplay of individuals. We are born into tribes and polities, and even in our innermost thoughts we never escape their influence. Enlightenment philosophers of every stripe, from at least Hobbes onward, emphasized the individuality of humans. But Aristotle's view that humans are inseparable from our tribes and communities is closer to where modern sociology and social psychology have brought us.

On the other hand, Aristotle's politics does not leave much room for individual freedom as we understand it, fundamental rights, and a politics rooted in consent that is ultimately most deeply rooted in equality. That tension between a politics of soulcraft and a politics of individual liberty has always remained part of our political tradition, and we see it in the newspapers every day. When liberals charge conservatives with selfishness, and when conservatives charge liberals with collectivism, they are debating Aristotle.

To summarize, then, some of the political principles America learned from Aristotle:

- Politics is an essential moral enterprise structuring our public life to encourage virtue and moral excellence.
- Being part of a political community is necessary to achieve the good life. The state exists for the purpose of helping people acquire that virtue and moral excellence.
- Rulers are not above the law and need to be held accountable.
- Politics negotiates the ongoing tension between the needs of the group and the liberty of individuals.

John Locke

Like Aristotle, Locke was a man of prodigious interests and talents: an Englishman working in the midst of political tumult in the seventeenth century, he wore many hats—a political and moral philosopher, a physician and political advisor, a public intellectual who made the case for the reasonableness of Christianity and pioneered new ideas on religious toleration and the separation between church and state.

His most important achievement, however, was as a father of classical liberalism. Today when we hear the word *liberal*, we understand it as a political or cultural or intellectual camp opposed to the conservative camp. But that is not what is meant by *classical liberalism*, the movement that created the foundation for American democracy and that both camps fit squarely within. For these reasons, no other individual played so great a role in shaping the views of the American founders as John Locke, who has fairly been called "America's philosopher."

Born in 1632, Locke attended the prestigious Christ Church, Oxford, and became the personal physician and close counselor to Lord Ashley, later the Earl of Shaftsbury, one of England's most prominent politicians. Shaftsbury not only allowed Locke to be at the center of political life; he played a vital role in Locke's intellectual journey away from political and religious authoritarianism and the near-absolute authority of kings toward liberalism and tolerance.[9]

Locke was an empiricist, an honest and balanced thinker, a man of moderate sensibilities. "He was a religious man; but he had no sympathy with fanaticism or with intemperate zeal," according to intellectual historian Frederick Copleston. "One does not look to him for brilliant extravaganzas or for flashes of genius; but one finds in him an absence of extremes and the presence of common sense."[10]

His common sense, however, led him to some revolutionary conclusions. One of those, from his *Essay Concerning Human Understanding*, is that knowledge comes mainly from our senses and our experience. That may seem obvious today, but it could— and did—help propel and justify the scientific revolution.

It also propelled a political revolution. Locke believed that knowledge is accessible but our capacity to know is not limitless, and on matters about which we have no certain knowledge, "we ought to regulate our assent, and moderate our persuasions." In

other words, we must make room for ongoing debate and disagreements on matters for which we cannot gain certainty. He
believed, further, that while human beings are rational and capable of moral excellence, they are also driven by appetites and
detestations, so laws are important checks on both. These concepts helped ground his views of politics. Locke knew that the
understanding one has of human nature and human knowledge
has profound practical effects. He was not building "a Castle in
the Air," to use his words, but rather a foundation upon which
politics must be based.

Which brings us to Locke's most important political work, his
*Second Treatise of Government: An Essay Concerning the True Origi-
nal Extent and End of Civil Government* in 1690. In it Locke argues
that (1) human beings are born free, (2) government should be
limited in its power, and (3) the power of government rests on the
consent of the governed. In our democratic age, it is easy to miss
how radical these principles sound, but in an age led by mon-
archs and aristocrats, these were both challenging and courageous
views to espouse. According to Locke, sovereignty rests with the
people, and political leaders are accountable to them. Only God,
not earthly governments, is deserving of absolute authority in our
lives. No mere human being can have the faultless knowledge or
perfect inspiration that could justify a natural right to rule others.

All of these concepts are commonplace today, but in Locke's
time they were revolutionary. He redefined the purpose of government by rooting it in human equality. Government was not
designed to enact the will of the aristocracy for its own designs;
instead government is for the sake of the people administered by
the government. For Locke, equality was a premise, not just an
aspiration. All human beings are free and equal to begin with. A

legitimate government is one designed to reflect the fact of human equality and to protect the rights that naturally flow from that fact. Equality and those rights precede the state. They are inherent, not granted by government; governments exist to protect and secure them. It is therefore in relation to the individual that the state is ultimately measured. In this respect, Locke marks a sharp break with Aristotle's political vision, which assessed regimes based on whether they were directed toward the common good, and points the way toward the kinds of political principles we now take for granted.

How does Locke reason his way from his seemingly simplistic premises to a robust and complex vision of government? He begins by going back in time before the creation of politics. Men and women resided in a state of nature before they consented to live under a government.[11] In this state of nature, we were ruled by the laws of nature, not individuals with the power to enforce civil law. Eventually, though, we came to see—because of defects in human nature, because of the accompanying vices, because of the need to regulate commerce—a need to give up some of our freedom in order to preserve what Locke referred to as life, liberty, and property. "The great and *chief end* . . . of men's uniting into common-wealths, and putting themselves under government, *is the preservation of their property*," Locke writes.[12] By *property* he meant all the basic prerogatives of life, not just material possessions. Without government and political society, liberty slips away.

Power is transferred to government, then, as a way to preserve the rights to which we are all equally entitled, but at the same time, there are strict limitations on the power of the state. That was the balance society needed to get right: government needed to be empowered but not all-powerful. Arbitrary and unlimited power is an even greater threat to individuals than the state of nature, according to Locke.

Not only are the powers of government limited, however; they are revocable. In the words of the political scientist C. B. Macpherson, summarizing Locke: "The authority of any government is conditional on its performing the functions for which it was entrusted with power."[13] And when the proper limits on the power of government are transgressed, then it is the government, not the people, that is in rebellion. This was precisely the ground in which the American Revolution was rooted.

It's difficult to overstate Locke's influence on the American founding. His commitment to ideals such as unalienable rights, limited government, and the separation of powers is plainly reflected in the Declaration of Independence and the Constitution, as well as in how the founders viewed human nature and political society.

Near the end of his life, Thomas Jefferson confessed, "As to the general principles of liberty and the rights of man in nature and in society, the doctrines of Locke, in his 'Essay concerning the true original extent and end of civil government,' and of [the seventeenth-century English theorist Algernon] Sidney in his 'Discourses on government,' may be considered as those generally approved by our fellow citizens of [Virginia], and of the US."[14] (Jefferson went even further in declaring, in his 1789 letter to John Trumbull, that he considered Locke, along with Francis Bacon and Isaac Newton, to be among the three greatest men who had ever lived.[15])

Where Locke perhaps most decisively split with Aristotle—and where as a general matter the modern philosophers differ from the classical ones—was regarding whether it is wise for politics and governments to take up the task of shaping souls and the inner lives of citizens.

Locke thought not. In *A Letter Concerning Toleration*, he wrote:

> But idolatry, say some, is a sin and therefore not to be tolerated. If they said it were therefore to be avoided, the inference were good. But it does not follow that because it is a sin it ought therefore to be punished by the magistrate. For it does not belong unto the magistrate to make use of his sword in punishing everything, indifferently, that he takes to be a sin against God.

Locke went on to say:

> Covetousness, uncharitableness, idleness, and many other things are sins by the consent of men, which yet no man ever said were to be punished by the magistrate. The reason is because they are not prejudicial to other men's rights, nor do they break the public peace of societies. Nay, even the sins of lying and perjury are nowhere punishable by laws; unless, in certain cases, in which the real turpitude of the thing and the offence against God are not considered, but only the injury done unto men's neighbours and to the commonwealth. And what if in another country, to a Mahometan or a Pagan prince, the Christian religion seem false and offensive to God; may not the Christians for the same reason, and after the same manner, be extirpated there?[16]

It's important to underscore here that Locke wasn't indifferent to the moral law, the need for an ethical society or a virtuous citizenry.

For him it was a matter of appropriateness and efficacy—about whether soulcraft was an appropriate task for government, and even if it was, how well the state could do the job, and at what cost.

Alan Ryan writes that Locke's purpose was to

> deny that government has any concern with spiritual matters; "property" is the shorthand term for our "external" goods—security against attack, the ability to make a living, freedom of movement, and the like—and sharply distinguished from a concern with our immortal souls. The latter is more important than the former, but Locke wants to protect our inner lives and our spiritual allegiances from the coercive interference of the state just because they are the most important parts of our lives.[17]

The reach and authority of government, then, should be circumscribed, at least for many of the key figures of the Enlightenment, the intellectual architects of classical liberalism, and the central figures in the first century of America's existence.

In summary, then, these are the political principles we gained from John Locke and classical liberalism:

- Human beings are born free and equal, and these qualities are inherent and therefore do not derive from the state.
- The power of government rests on the consent of the governed; as a result, restraints on government are required to maintain its proper functioning.
- Government is measured by how it protects the individual and her rights—and because arbitrary and

unrestrained state power is a threat to the individual, government should be limited in its power.

- The state should not be engaged in the business of shaping souls.
- There exists an ongoing tension, and hence a political debate, in assessing when the proper limits on the power of government are transgressed.

Regarding the last principle, this question was never simply settled. And the place of moral questions—and of matters of character and virtue—in politics remained a source of tension and dispute in the practical political life of every free society, very much including ours. When social conservatives and progressives, in their different ways, argue that government cannot *avoid* legislating morality, it is Locke they are arguing with.

In fact, core moral questions proved inescapable in the political life of our country, in no small part because the question of slavery in America remained unsettled in the wake of the founding and was a moral stain on the life of the early republic. As American politics came gradually to grasp that this question would prove unavoidable, the nature of the difference between political and moral questions itself became a heated controversy.

No one approached this controversy with greater depth of thought and care than Abraham Lincoln.

Abraham Lincoln

One of my favorite responsibilities as director of "strategery"—as we referred to the Office of Strategic Initiatives in the White House—was to organize meetings for President Bush with public intellectuals, biographers, and historians, including several Lincoln scholars.

Contrary to the caricature popularized by his critics, President Bush was a voracious reader, especially of biographies, and during his presidency he read fourteen biographies of Lincoln alone. He once called me to discuss Richard Carwardine's *Lincoln: A Life of Purpose and Power*, which captivated the president, and he became friends with at least one of the Lincoln biographers I introduced him to, Ronald C. White. On the space on the wall in the Oval Office reserved for the president's most influential predecessor, Bush hung a portrait of Lincoln. And understandably so. "The life-story of Abraham Lincoln became one with the life-story of the American people," Lord Charnwood wrote in his masterly 1917 biography of Lincoln.[18]

That life story is by now familiar to many Americans. Lincoln was born in 1809 in Kentucky before his family eventually made their way to Indiana and then Illinois. A man of very little formal education—less than a year all told—Lincoln was an autodidact, a voracious reader of the King James Bible and John Bunyan, the poetry of Lord Byron and Robert Burns, Shakespeare's plays and *Robinson Crusoe*, William Blackstone's *Commentaries on the Law*, and Edward Gibbon's *Decline and Fall of the Roman Empire*. For him, it has been said, "literature and life were inseparable."[19] He became a successful lawyer but eventually entered the profession he loved, politics, where he served in the House of Representatives for a single two-year term.

After a hiatus from politics, Lincoln was motivated to reenter it in response to the Supreme Court's Dred Scott decision, which permitted the extension of slavery into all the new territories of the Union. He ran for the Senate in 1858 as a member of the newly established Republican Party, challenging Stephen Douglas. It was an election that centered on and clarified the most urgent issue facing the republic: whether slavery would be accepted or abolished. Douglas argued for acceptance, under the banner of "popular sovereignty"; Lincoln argued for eventual abolition, insisting that slavery was incompatible with the self-evident truth and defining moral principle of the American founding: all men are created equal.

Lincoln lost in a close race, with the state legislature, dominated by Democrats, deciding the outcome. But Lincoln impressed people with the way he conducted himself during the campaign, and he was glad he had entered the contest since "it gave me a hearing on the great and durable questions of the age."[20]

Against long odds and with a notably short resume, Lincoln ran for president in 1860, winning with less than 40 percent of the popular vote in a fractured field. Speaking to journalists the day after the election, he told them, "Well boys, your troubles are over now, mine have just begun."[21] Within three months of Lincoln's election, seven Southern states had seceded from the Union. And within a month after his inauguration, South Carolina fired on Fort Sumter.

Describing the lead-up to the Civil War, Lincoln, in his second inaugural address, put it this way: "Both parties deprecated war, but one of them would *make* war rather than let the nation survive, and the other would *accept* war rather than let it perish. And the war came." Victory for the North, and the abolition of slavery, came only after many more years and far more bloodshed than anyone, including Lincoln, had anticipated.

After easily winning reelection in 1864, Lincoln was assassinated the following year by John Wilkes Booth. His death was met by an outpouring of grief, even in parts of the South, and Lincoln immediately entered, and has never left, the American pantheon.

Lincoln was a complicated and deeply impressive human being: magnanimous and generous, compassionate and incorruptible, seemingly free of personal pettiness and maliciousness. "He did not mark down the names of those who had not supported him, or nurse grudges, or hold resentments, or retaliate against 'enemies,'" according to the Lincoln biographer William Lee Miller. "Indeed, he tried not to have enemies, not to 'plant thorns.'"[22] Neither personal nor professional scandal ever touched or tainted his life.

Lincoln was blessed with wit and a sense of humor, even as he was cursed with melancholy. He was a marvelous storyteller and charming raconteur—it was said Lincoln would "brighten like a lit lantern" in conversation[23]—but also inward looking, intensely ambitious, enigmatic. "Though he was an indefatigable conversationalist, could be excellent company, and dominated gatherings through his storytelling," according to Richard Carwardine, "even his near friends encountered reticence and secrecy, and most judged that he 'never told all he felt.'"[24]

Lincoln was also given the gift of a brilliant, retentive mind. "His reasoning through logic, analogy and comparison was unerring and deadly," according to his law partner William Herndon.[25] Arguably, too, he was the greatest of all American writers. While he never wrote a book or even kept a private diary or journal, his words are literally etched in stone at the west end of the National Mall in Washington, DC.

What matters most, however, isn't the beautifully crafted eloquence of Lincoln's words but their content. He put forward a set of arguments about the true nature of the American Revolution, arguing that the Declaration of Independence and its claim of equality were the "sheet anchor of American republicanism," the embodiment of the American creed. "I have never had a feeling politically that did not spring from the sentiments embodied in the Declaration of Independence," Lincoln admitted.[26]

To those, like Stephen Douglas, who argued that free citizens in the territories could vote for slavery if it was an expression of the popular will, Lincoln said, emphatically, no. As the historian Charles Strozier put it, "Popular sovereignty was a valid democratic practice, but not if it is contradicted by fundamental law. Basic human rights could not be voted up or down by a majority."[27]

The question America was forced to grapple with was whether the nation was at its core a procedural democracy or a polity committed to certain ideals. Lincoln insisted on interpreting the Constitution, which is primarily a *procedural* charter, through the lens of the Declaration of Independence, which put forward a *philosophical and moral* proposition. The pace and the precise manner in which slavery would be put on the "road to extinction" was a prudential matter, but Lincoln never budged from his belief that slavery could not extend into new territories and that slavery was a moral evil.

For Lincoln, the black man was a man; all men are created equal and have an equal claim to just treatment; just treatment is based on intrinsic worth; and our intrinsic worth is based on being made in the image of the Creator. Lincoln not only claimed those beliefs as his; he insisted that they reflected the views of the American founders as well. After quoting the "all men are created equal" line in the Declaration of Independence, Lincoln said:

> This was their majestic interpretation of the economy of the Universe. This was their lofty, and wise, and noble understanding of the justice of the Creator to His creatures. Yes, gentlemen, to *all* His creatures, to the whole great family of man. In their enlightened belief, nothing stamped with the Divine image and likeness was sent into the world to be trodden on, and degraded, and imbruted by its fellows. They grasped not only the whole race of man then living, but they reached forward and seized upon the farthest posterity. They erected a beacon to guide their children and their children's children, and the countless myriads who should inhabit the earth in other ages.[28]

The degree to which Lincoln correctly interpreted the views of the American founders remains a point of debate among scholars. Some, like Garry Wills, argue that Lincoln essentially refounded the nation—that he "revolutionized the Revolution"—while others, like Harry Jaffa, believe he clarified the intent of the founders.[29] In any event, America was a profoundly different nation—politically, philosophically, and morally—because of Lincoln.

What can be said about Lincoln, which can't be said about either Aristotle or Locke, is that he was a statesman who faced a most extraordinary crisis. He wasn't primarily a philosopher, though his mastery of political ideas was profound. He was primarily a *practitioner* of politics, who translated principles into action and gave them the force of arms. He took certain philosophical concepts—some from classical Greece (e.g., prudence), some from the Enlightenment (equality), some from Judaism and Christianity (intrinsic human worth)—and engrafted them so as to fit the circumstances and meet the challenges of his time. Lincoln is revered by most, and cursed by some, because he was preeminently a man of action. He would not allow the nation he led to exist in the service of false ideals.

Though Lincoln's words and ideas were important, perhaps as great a legacy is the manner in which he practiced politics and comported himself. He combined strength with forbearance, a ferocious will to win the war with restraint in victory. Lincoln fully understood the moral stakes involved in the Civil War even as he resisted the temptation to treat Southerners as lacking in any human dignity or human worth.

Lord Charnwood, arguably Lincoln's greatest biographer, said of him:

> For perhaps not many conquerors, and certainly few successful statesmen, have escaped the tendency of power to harden or at least to narrow their human sympathies; but in this man a natural wealth of tender compassion became richer and more tender while in the stress of deadly conflict he developed an astounding strength.[30]

Having prevailed in a great struggle, he showed humanity and eschewed casual cruelty. He was willing to concede that his side was not perfect and the other side was not unmitigated evil.

It's hard to imagine anyone but Lincoln saying at the beginning of the war, "We are not enemies, but friends," and by the end being able to say, "With malice toward none, with charity for all, with firmness in the right, as God gives us to see the right, let us strive on to finish the work we are in, to bind up the nation's wounds." We could surely use those sensibilities in our time, when such grace and largeness of spirit are in such short supply.

At the end of his biography, Lord Charnwood wrote, "His own intense experience of the weakness of democracy did not sour him, nor would any similar experience of later times have been likely to do so." He was too much of a patriot for that.

Lincoln's contribution to American politics, then, includes the following:

- The US Constitution and our laws and traditions are built on the foundation of the ideals expressed in the Declaration of Independence.
- The heart of the Declaration of Independence is expressed in its second sentence: "We hold these truths to be self-evident, that all men are created equal, that they are endowed by their Creator with certain unalienable Rights, that among these are Life, Liberty and the pursuit of Happiness."
- Fundamental human rights should never be decided by majority rule.
- Passionately fighting for a just cause and treating enemies of that just cause with dignity and forbearance are not incompatible.

Lincoln lived in a much more riven and difficult time than ours, yet he refused to give up on his belief that politics could right certain wrongs. He didn't withdraw from public life. He didn't become consumed by hatred or cynicism. He never stopped seeking the better angels of our nature, in himself and also in his opponents.

Neither should we.

PREVENTING RUIN

People get involved in politics for all sorts of different reasons. Some like the challenge of campaigns. Others feel a strong affinity to a political party, which connects them with like-minded people in pursuit of a common purpose. Still others are drawn to politics because they enjoy the adulation of the crowd. Some are attracted to power. And many do it because they care about a set of issues that politics can advance. Often it's a combination of many of the above.

One of the main attractions of politics for me has been the power of ideas to shape history. I have always been intrigued by people who respect ideas and take them seriously, by those who sought to "reopen the channels of communication between the world of thought and the seat of power," in the words of John F. Kennedy. Aristotle, Locke, and Lincoln not only inhabited both worlds; they deepened our understanding of them.

Aristotle, Locke, and Lincoln lived in different centuries, social circumstances, and historical settings. Like all of us, they were to some degree imprisoned by the moments in which they lived, reacting to the challenges and opportunities that defined their times. But they also saw farther than that, and so offer us far more than insights on their day. They offer timeless wisdom about politics, and the combination of their three very different visions in particular can help us see more deeply into our society and our time.

One of the things I have learned from studying their lives is that politics is an art, not a science, and that the application of human ideals to human society is an immensely complicated task. No one ever gets it exactly right.

As we have seen, Aristotle, Locke, and Lincoln held divergent views on, among other things, the precise role and even the best forms of government. (Aristotle had a much darker view of democracy than Locke and Lincoln, though the latter two were aware of the traps that attend self-government.) Aristotle and Locke disagreed about the degree to which politics should be the work of shaping souls, with Lincoln showing us how the best of each man's insights can be melded together in practice.

But for our purposes what all three held in common is even more important than their differences: their conviction that politics is a prerequisite for human thriving; that the failure of politics expresses itself in moral, economic, and social ruin; that politics needs to be rooted in a realistic conception of the human person and a correct reading of human nature; and that the qualities to prize in statesmen are prudence, wise judgment, and discernment. They all worried about the passions, zealotry, and mob rule. And they knew that politics, when done correctly, allows humans to flourish in areas beyond politics.

People can choose, if they wish, to go through life belittling politics and convincing themselves that it is a low, degraded, and corrupt enterprise, one that doesn't work and never will. But that attitude is very much at odds with the lessons we can draw from our exceptional inheritance (of which these three men stand as particularly glittering and illustrious examples); and it is at odds with history and reality.

It would be easy to look at these three exemplars and think

they have nothing to do with what we now think of as politics in America. But that would be nothing more than an indictment of how we have come to think about politics. Properly understood, politics has everything to do with Aristotle's concern for human flourishing, with Locke's insistence that the legitimacy of government must be rooted in the equality of the human person, and with Lincoln's commitment to Locke's proposition of equality precisely for the sake of Aristotle's concern with the integrity of the soul.

When we flirt with the possibility of deviating from this foundation, what is at stake? It may seem that the struggles and suffering that are happening in the shadows of America's affluence—the "cocaine babies" I learned about early in my own time in government, orphaned and abandoned children, economically disadvantaged students attending failing schools, people trapped in poverty, the chronically unemployed, victims of gang violence and mass shootings, women who have been sexually assaulted and victims of domestic violence, inhumane prison conditions, homelessness, trauma experienced by returning war veterans—are far removed from the realm of political ideas, from the philosophies and eras of people like Aristotle and Locke and Lincoln. Yet those people's fate and those men's ideas are inextricably interwoven.

One kind of political culture takes the fate and equality of each human person to heart; another sees humans as expendable or of differing worth. One political culture attempts to hold its leaders to account for decisions affecting even the weakest; another regards might as right. One kind of political culture teaches an ethic of responsibility; another promotes dependency.

Every generation has to decide whether it will continue

America's noble experiment in ordered liberty or allow the foundation our ancestors built to fracture. Today we are witnessing cracks forming and spreading, due in part to a president who delights in demonization, who himself embodies an ethic of cruelty and selfishness, and whose corruptions are borderless.

Are we ready to do the hard work of repairing these fissures, of firming up our foundation, of taking the necessary steps to make us a more perfect union? This is the question before us. The remainder of this book is my attempt to show how we can move forward.

CHAPTER 4

Politics and Faith

I'm gonna break [Pat] Buchanan's neck and leave him in the snow, without any fingerprints."

Those words, followed by a loud cackle, might sound like they came from a mafia don. In this case, however, they were said by Ralph Reed during a meeting with me and one other person at the offices of Empower America, leading up to the 1996 Republican primary.

Reed—at that time the boyish-looking, smooth-talking leader of the Christian Coalition—had been publicly respectful of Buchanan but privately opposed him and was a de facto supporter of Robert Dole. As Nina Easton pointed out in her book *Gang of Five*, Reed was not about to let a movement he had helped develop be hijacked by Buchanan.

Buchanan's stances were protectionist and nativist, his rhetoric divisive and exclusive, which was at odds with what Reed believed a successful Christian political movement should look like. And Buchanan's eagerness to weigh in on issues like the Confederate flag, which inflamed racial tensions, made Reed uncomfortable.

He wanted to refashion the evangelical movement away from the judgmental, off-putting attitudes of Jerry Falwell Sr. and Reed's boss, Pat Robertson. Yet Reed had to be careful, because Buchanan, although a Catholic, inspired a lot of evangelicals. He was a culture warrior par excellence.

In the end, Dole won the nomination. Buchanan's candidacy failed, but much of his agenda and approach to politics would eventually be embraced by, of all people, Donald Trump—a foul-mouthed, non-church-attending former casino owner and reality television star who once endorsed partial-birth abortion and was convincingly accused of paying hush money to cover up an affair with a porn star, which took place after his third wife gave birth to their son.

But not only did Buchanan win in the long run against Ralph Reed's 1996 vision of how Christians should engage politics; today Reed is one of Trump's key allies, a bridge to the white evangelical world. The evangelical world has in turn rallied around Trump, supporting him for president in even greater numbers than it did George W. Bush, a lifelong conservative who spoke easily and openly about his relationship with Christ. As a result, white evangelicals got a seat at the table of power, something that in his life Jesus never did. But this ascent to power has come at a devastating cost to evangelicalism's moral integrity and credibility, damage that might take generations to heal, if it ever does. To put the case bluntly, evangelicals and others were correct to say that religion should inform politics—but they let down their guard against politics corrupting religion.

What happened?

PROMISE AND PERIL

From Aristotle we learned that politics is both a necessary and an inherently moral enterprise since it is centered on a vision of what is good and what we should aspire to. Traditionally, many Americans have looked to Christianity to provide the language, values, and aspirations for how we define what is good and right for our nation. And so it's not at all surprising that in America, which throughout its history has been one of the more religious countries in the world, religion and politics would be intertwined.

Actually, "intertwined" is something of an understatement, because the dynamic between religion and politics in the United States is unique. Inspired by John Locke's ideas of tolerance and the limits of government, which were adapted and implemented here in America mostly through the creative work of James Madison in the Bill of Rights' First Amendment, America's combination of the separation between religion and politics alongside its protection of religious minorities has made it the exception among developed nations: a flourishing religious culture in which no one sect serves as the "established" faith for the nation.

This balancing act is one of our greatest achievements.

Still, precisely because of religions' centrality to our national culture, when religion itself is corrupted, it creates problems that extend beyond religion. It seeps into our political and cultural life—as we have seen in current events.

In this chapter, unlike the previous ones, I will be donning two hats, wearing my religious hat in addition to my political one. As is true for many Americans, I cannot easily separate these subjects, since what drives my sense of right, wrong, duty, wisdom, goodness, and care for others cannot be neatly separated into buckets, one marked "sacred" and the other "secular." To get our politics right, it helps to get our religion right—and it is clear to many of us right now that neither side is getting things quite "right."

Worries about the influence between religion and politics have been with us from the beginning of our history, including our recent history, and they go in both directions. From their inception in the 1970s, groups like the Moral Majority were viewed as judgmental, censorious, and selective in their moral concerns. Critics of the religious Right feared it wanted to impose a theocracy and was willing to use faith as a partisan cudgel. Dispensing God's grace and redemptive love wasn't the real agenda, critics claimed; it was about gaining and holding raw political power.

Over the last few years—particularly during the Trump years—concerns about how well faith and politics mix have been reinforced and deepened. Those who want there to be a great, even unbridgeable distance between faith and politics come from two very different points on the spectrum. There are some, often but not exclusively secularists, who believe religion is a grave threat to politics; and there are some, almost all of whom are Christians, who worry that entanglement with politics is doctrinally problematic and will corrupt faith.

Those in the former category make several arguments, including invoking the history of religious wars. Following Europe's bloody wars of religion, Enlightenment figures such as John Locke (whom we met earlier in the book) and others in England and on the European continent argued that religion and politics needed to be separated, that (at most) faith belonged in the private but not the public sphere, and that mixing the two invariably leads to conflict. This was an understandable response to a particular historical moment.

The underlying danger, from this perspective, is that religious passions stir up political passions, which are difficult enough to control. Those who are religious believe they represent God's side while their opponents represent Satan's, which makes accommodation nearly impossible. It frames political disputes as between the children of light and the children of darkness, between the righteous and the malevolent. Furthermore, this argument goes, religion is a license to discriminate, an engine of intolerance, repression, and mindless moralism.

From the other direction are those who insist that politics should be kept at a distance from religion to protect the purity of faith. Their views are rooted in part in theology, the belief that Jesus's kingdom was not of this world and we are therefore called to be separated from it. Jesus was not a political figure, after all, and neither should we be.

This argument rests on the belief that the primary Christian contribution is to be a model for another kingdom, embodying "kingdom values" and not becoming entangled with the compromises inherent in dealing with the kingdoms of this world. They believe that if we take Jesus's words literally we must abide an inevitable tension with life in this world, so the involvement needs to be minimized. Otherwise we are in danger of giving up Christian distinctiveness.

These concerns have some legitimacy; it's not as if they have been invented out of nothing. Sometimes religion *has* had a pernicious influence on politics, and sometimes being involved in politics *has* damaged the integrity of faith. But there is also a different view to consider on this question—a more positive and constructive way to view the involvement of faith in public life.

BUILDING ON A FIRM FOUNDATION

Despite the fact that our nation was formed right after Europe's religious wars, most of the American founders—Washington, Jefferson, Madison, Hamilton, Franklin, and others—argued that religion was essential in providing a moral basis for a free society. Typical was the sentiment of John Adams:

> We have no Government armed with Power capable of contending with human Passions unbridled by morality and Religion. Avarice, Ambition, Revenge or Gallantry, would break the strongest Cords of our Constitution as a Whale goes through a Net. Our Constitution is designed only for a moral and religious People. It is wholly inadequate to the government of any other.[1]

Religion was, in the words of Jefferson, "a supplement to law in the government of men" and the "alpha and omega of the moral law."[2] Washington put it this way: "Of all the dispositions and habits which lead to political prosperity, religion and morality are indispensable supports . . . And let us with caution indulge the supposition that morality can be maintained without religion."[3]

To be sure, the key figures in the American founding opposed theocracy and wanted neutrality toward different religious sects. They supported the prohibition on religious establishment in the Constitution's First Amendment. Yet they also believed religion played a useful private *and* public role and was even an essential element in education. There is simply no disputing that religious faith shaped our national ideals, from the Puritans through the Declaration of Independence to the work of Lincoln and Martin Luther King Jr.

Of course, simply because the founders made these claims doesn't mean they were correct. It could also be that they were right in their time but their arguments no longer apply in our time; that religious faith was a positive force at the founding but has become less of one today.

Let's see if their arguments hold up in today's world, then. The strongest case for religion in public life comes from the moral instruction needed in guiding our politics—religion helps ground politics in morality. Without this grounding, it's more difficult to appeal to fixed moral points. It has never been clear to me, for example, how one can make a persuasive case for justice and the moral good—even for the proposition that all men and women are created equal—without an appeal to God and transcendent truth, since it's not clear what the grounding for truth would be.

My point isn't that atheists can't be good people; clearly they can, and many prove that every day. Many, in fact, live lives of greater moral integrity than people of faith. I'm making a rather different point, which is that it's difficult for them to offer a compelling case for inherent human dignity and worth. What is their argument against capriciousness and injustice, tyranny, and the will to power, absent a Creator?

I have posed to atheist friends of mine—including the late Christopher Hitchens, who authored one of the most popular caustic attacks on God, *God Is Not Great: How Religion Poisons Everything*—several interlocking questions. How does one create a system of justice and make the case against, say, slavery, if you begin with three propositions: one, the universe is created by chance; two, it will end in nothing; and three, there is no external source of authority to which to resort?

Christopher was a polemicist and a man of dazzling intelligence, and I found him to be more charming and less abrasive in person than in print. (One of the more enjoyable conversations we had was about faith, C. S. Lewis, and the British journalist and later convert to Christianity Malcolm Muggeridge.)

Christopher would typically respond to the question I posed to him by challenging the person asking it to name one ethical statement made, or one ethical action performed, by a believer that could not have been uttered or done by a nonbeliever. He would then ask them to consider all of the wicked statements made and evil actions performed by people precisely *because* of religious faith.

Of course, it's perfectly legitimate to point out that religion can be corrupted and has been used for awful ends. And I have readily conceded that nonbelievers can act ethically and do so all the time. But that still doesn't explain what a nontheistic moral code would be grounded in.

Let me press the point further: If you were a materialist or a relativist, why would you have any confidence that your beliefs were rooted in anything permanent or that they applied to you and to others? How would you respond to a Nietzschean who said, "Your belief is fine for you, but it is simply not binding to me. God is dead—and I choose to follow my Will to Power. You may not agree, but there is no philosophical or moral ground on which you can make your stand."

How do you get from the "is" to the "ought"? How do you avoid the trap laid out by Ivan Karamazov: If God does not exist, "everything is permitted"?

Even supposing human beings have moral instincts and a moral sense based on human evolution and biology, why would you choose to follow them? We have lots of instincts—some noble and some base. Why would you choose the more noble ones, like cooperation and sympathy, tolerance and fair play, instead of, say, using power against those you have authority over? Why not rig the game to advance your own self-interests? Why not cheat on your wife if you derive pleasure from it? "When all that says 'it is good' has been debunked," C. S. Lewis said, "what says 'I want' remains."[4]

Steve Hayner, the former president of Columbia Theological Seminary and a spiritual mentor of mine who passed away in 2015, told me something that adds an important layer to this discussion. We believe we have worth because we are created in God's image, he said. But even more basic is the declaration that we have value simply because God values us.

Gold is valuable because someone values it, not because there is something about gold that has intrinsic worth. Sure, gold is aesthetically beautiful and has particular physical qualities that set it apart (it is highly conductive, for example, and noncorroding). But gold would not be valuable if it were not thought to be so by someone. In this case, value is attributed to gold by us and would lose its value if we collectively decided it no longer had value. But human beings are of worth because we are valued by God. Indeed, Christians believe God demonstrates the value of humanity by his continuing involvement with us.

It is God's *attributive* quality of worth that underlies Christian and Jewish anthropology. Humanly derived values create comparative worth, which opens the door to an economic or utilitarian assessment of the value of an individual. Divinely attributed values convey intrinsic worth. According to Hayner, our worth was not derived from culture or circumstances. Here, worth comes from understanding all people as precious in God's sight.

Antitheists disagree that we have worth because human beings are precious in God's sight. They treat religious beliefs as mere superstition—and for some, as something less than knowledge and therefore having nothing to contribute to political philosophy or to our understanding of human nature. But it is one thing to argue that God doesn't exist; it is quite another to insist that faith can offer nothing of use, that it "poisons everything," to use a Hitchens phrase—that it can't offer insights into the human condition. Augustine and Aquinas, Jonathan Edwards and Reinhold Niebuhr, Maimonides and Rabbi Joshua Heschel, Mahatma Gandhi and Avicenna, and countless others, prove otherwise. (To be fair, I have friends who are atheists who don't accept supernaturalism as a warrant for moral beliefs but still value the moral insights and arguments of religious thinkers who make what they deem to be rational claims. As one of them put it to me, "We wouldn't dream of tossing Jesus or Augustine in the trash.")

In sum, then: without an appeal to transcendent truth and authority, there is nothing one ultimately can anchor morality in; and if politics is stripped of morality, it's merely a power game. Politics, without fixed moral points, easily devolves into unchecked power, from which abuses result. And theology, once considered the queen of the disciplines, can deepen our understanding of public life and the common good. Those who criticize religion as an inherently baleful influence on politics would do well to understand, as Nietzsche did, just how ugly and terrifying a world without moral absolutes would be.

It needs to be said that many thinkers have wrestled conscientiously and intelligently with how to find moral grounding without God, arguing that our knowledge of right and wrong is innate in us. "Religion gets its morality from humans," according to Hitchens. "We know that we can't get along if we permit perjury, theft, murder, rape. All societies at all times, well before the advent of monotheism, certainly, have forbidden it."[5]

I don't find their efforts ultimately persuasive, but this book is not the place to dive deeper into these ageless disputes. Suffice to say that, for the faithful explicitly and even for many secular people implicitly, religion provides an indispensable moral true north, and it would not be reasonable to expect all these Americans to leave their compasses at home.

As for those of the Christian faith who insist that their theology argues against political involvement—who argue for segregating the "sacred" from the "secular" and that Christians should be, in the words of the historian of religion Darryl Hart, "occupied with a world to come rather than the passing and temporal affairs of this world"[6]—I would respectfully suggest they are distorting things to a rather serious degree.

Citizenship is an important Christian concept. For those of the Christian faith, the ultimate allegiance is to the City of God, to borrow a phrase from Saint Augustine. "Our citizenship is in heaven," the Apostle Paul wrote to the church in Philippi. "And we eagerly await a Savior from there, the Lord Jesus Christ." But as the theologian Timothy Keller pointed out to me, in the book of Acts Paul regularly refers to and relies on his Roman citizenship, which came with both rights and duties. (At the time Roman citizenship was restricted and taken quite seriously, a "coveted treasure" in the words of the New Testament scholar Sean A. Adams.)[7] "That is something like what we see in Jeremiah 29, where the Jews who were ultimately citizens of Jerusalem were called to be excellent citizens of Babylon," according to Keller. "It is clear as can be that, while our ultimate allegiance is to the City Above, that should make us the very best citizens of our earthly cities."[8]

Moreover, the Christian faith, as I understand it, teaches that theological truths apply to all of God's creation; that Christianity was never meant to be privatized; and that the biblical narrative is of God's active involvement in human affairs. Whatever one thinks about the Christian story, it does not portray a God who is distant, removed, and remote, indifferent to and disengaged from our lives or the life of this world. God clearly wanted to instruct us about how we should live in this life by participating in the human drama, not just as the author of it but as an actor in the drama.

FAITH WITHOUT WORKS IS DEAD

The God of Judaism and Christianity requires us to care for justice, and politics is a realm where that plays out. If Christians care about justice, then, they need to be involved with politics.

The biblical prophet Jeremiah tells us to seek the welfare of the city to which we have been exiled and pray to the Lord on its behalf, for in its prosperity we shall prosper. Withdrawing from an arena where human rights are contested—where the welfare of the city is decided—isn't a serious option. I would say the formulation of Rav Aharon Lichtenstein applies to the whole of scripture: "The Torah is neither world-accepting nor world-rejecting. It is world-redeeming."[9] The Jewish term *tikkun olam* means "to repair the world."

Christians in despair over the state of the world often miss the full picture. There is in fact much in America that is going right on a daily basis, in ways so common as to be forgotten. We take for granted, far more than we should, that by many measures we are living in the most privileged nation on earth during the best time to be alive in human history. And contrary to the impression left by some on the religious Right, the United States in the twenty-first century is not the Roman Empire under Nero, when, according to the Roman historian Tacitus, "Nero set up as the culprits and punished with utmost refinement of cruelty a class hated for their abominations, who are commonly called Christians. . . . Besides being put to death they were made to serve as objects of amusement; they were clad in hides of beasts and torn to death by dogs; others were crucified."[10] Yes, Christians are losing some cultural debates, but it is silly to describe our plight as if we were being fed to the dogs.

As for those who counsel retreating from politics: those who devalue the importance of politics tend to be those who live in luxury and safety, where systemic injustice is a distant reality, unseen and unfelt by those living in comfortable neighborhoods. "It is hard for those who live near a Police Station / To believe in the triumph of violence," T. S. Eliot wrote in his poem "Choruses from 'The Rock.'"

The temptation to retreat from politics goes aground when it hits this historical truth: America and the world have been made tangibly better and more just because Americans of faith took their beliefs into politics.

Let's first note the countless acts of kindness and charity by individuals motivated by faith who have helped the homeless, drug and alcohol addicts, single mothers and children of prisoners, the elderly and infirmed, victims of natural disaster, the poor and hungry, refugees and those trapped in slavery and sexual trafficking around the world, and more. According to the Pew Research Center, "people who are highly religious are more engaged with their extended families, more likely to volunteer, more involved in their communities and generally happier with the way things are going in their lives."[11] Other studies show that the religious among us are more likely to give to charities than those who do not identify with a faith tradition.[12]

But I have in mind as well great acts of compassion by government. For example, the global AIDS and malaria initiative is President George W. Bush's greatest legacy; more than 13 million people are on lifesaving antiretroviral treatment as a consequence. This was a policy that came about in response to human sympathies that were shaped in large part by the faith of Mr. Bush; some of his key advisors, including Michael Gerson, who was a senior policy advisor and chief speechwriter to President Bush and a committed evangelical Christian; and the rock star Bono, who worked with the president to combat AIDS. ("I've become very fond of him," Bono said of Bush. "Underneath his armor, there's passion, compassion. He has it.")[13]

I have in mind, too, movements for justice, including the abolitionist, labor, and pro-life movements, as well as the civil rights movement.

Martin Luther King Jr. was not just a civil rights activist; he was a reverend—pastor of the Dexter Avenue Baptist Church in Montgomery, Alabama, as well as a graduate of Crozer Theological Seminary and Boston University, where he received his PhD in systematic theology. Dr. King was also author of one of the landmark documents in American history, Letter from Birmingham Jail.

Written in 1963, it was addressed to white clergymen from Birmingham who believed King's efforts to overthrow segregation were "untimely." They counseled patience. They wanted the issue to be waged in the courtrooms rather than on the streets. These ministers were more concerned about civil rights protesters than the injustice the protesters were seeking to rectify.

In his nearly six-thousand-word point-by-point rebuttal, King argued that one has not only a legal but a moral responsibility to obey just laws—but conversely, one has a moral responsibility to disobey unjust laws. "Now, what is the difference between the two?" King asked. "How does one determine whether a law is just or unjust?" To which he answered thus:

> A just law is a man-made code that squares with the moral law or the law of God. An unjust law is a code that is out of harmony with the moral law. To put it in the terms of St. Thomas Aquinas, an unjust law is a human law that is not rooted in eternal law and natural law. Any law that uplifts human personality is just. Any law that degrades human personality is unjust. All segregation statutes are unjust because segregation distorts the soul and damages the personality.[14]

The dignity and worth of the human personality, King believed—as did Lincoln a century before him, and the American founders a century before *him*—were God given. (John F. Kennedy, one of the most revered figures among liberals and Democrats, declared in his inaugural address that "the rights of man come not from the generosity of the state but from the hand of God.")

It was religious faith that gave the civil rights movement its moral force. And it is religious faith that, at its best, provides ideals that transcend different cultures and allows us to stand in judgment of all cultures, including our own. Any movement for social justice depends on a set of values to define it.

It should be pointed out that King's letter was written by a Christian who believed in justice, but it was sent to Christians who were arguing that we *delay* justice. Which again underscores the point that religion can sometimes be a force for social good, and sometimes not. It depends on the wisdom, integrity, and courage of those who interpret and act on the scriptures. The devil can quote scripture for his own purposes, as Shakespeare put it; and all of us can cherry-pick from history to make very nearly whatever point we want. A fair reading of history is that Christians have opposed and been implicated in countless social evils. The record has always been mixed and remains so to this very day. But one must also admit that in many instances moral progress in our history was begun by courageous religious people doing what they thought God was calling them to do.

WHAT WENT WRONG?

As someone who has spent much of his life sympathetic to the positive role faith can play in political life, I sometimes feel the Trump presidency has very nearly been an outright repudiation of my views: not about whether politics *can* benefit from the influence of the Christian religion, but whether in reality it usually *does*; whether, in the practical outworking of things, both politics and the Christian witness are now made worse by people of faith actively involving themselves in politics.

I've harbored these concerns on and off for the last several decades. I have long been troubled by what I perceived as the subordination of Christianity to partisan ideology—the ease with which people took something sacred and turned it into a blunt political weapon. I saw this happen time and again through the years, always hoping that these temptations and abuses would recede and give way to a movement dedicated to justice and human dignity, one that stood in judgment of all political parties and ideologies and that was beholden to none. But Jerry Falwell Sr. gave way to Jerry Falwell Jr., Billy Graham gave way to Franklin Graham, and things are now worse, not better. The Trump era has utterly discredited significant parts of the American evangelical movement.[15]

Most people miss what was most troubling about the 2016 election cycle. It is not merely the fact that Trump won four-fifths of white evangelicals in the 2016 election against a candidate, Hillary Clinton, who was advocating policies they considered inimical to their beliefs. What is much worse and more troubling is that so many of them supported Mr. Trump in the *Republican* primaries, when there were more than a dozen candidates who were, by any reasonable standard that ought to matter to evangelicals, light-years better than Trump. I would go so far as to say it's very nearly impossible to defend even a single evangelical vote for Trump in the Republican primary, at least if evangelicals genuinely cared for the values they purport to represent.

Yet Trump not only did well with evangelicals; he won a plurality of evangelical votes in key early contests in New Hampshire, South Carolina, and Nevada. He garnered significant support on

"Super Tuesday." And by April 2016 he was the preferred candidate of more than a third of weekly churchgoers.[16] Trump could not have won the GOP nomination without the Christian vote.

A conservative friend who is generally very supportive of Christianity told me that the real danger for evangelical Christianity is that "it becomes a vehicle for resentments of middle-class white America," adding that "the church may become a voice for the resentments of the strong in the country when in fact it should focus on helping the weak."

As for evangelical leaders: what we saw from most was not pained, reluctant, qualified expressions of support for Trump—support based only on the fact that his opponent in the 2016 election was a committed liberal, Hillary Clinton. I would disagree with that stance even as I could acknowledge it's a defensible one.

What we have seen instead—from prominent evangelical figures like Jerry Falwell Jr., Franklin Graham, James Dobson, Tony Perkins, Eric Metaxas, Robert Jeffress, the former Baptist minister Mike Huckabee, and others—are defenses of Trump that range from rhapsodic to ridiculous. One illustration: Jerry Falwell Jr., president of one of the largest Christian colleges in the world, said that in Trump evangelicals had found their "dream president."[17] He insists that Trump is a Churchillian figure,[18] "one of the greatest visionaries of our time" who "lives a life of loving and helping others as Jesus taught in the New Testament."[19] Falwell Jr. added that Donald Trump has "single-handedly changed the definition of what behavior is 'presidential' from phony, failed & rehearsed to authentic, successful & down to earth."[20]

We all know—presumably in their quiet and more reflective moments *they* all know—that if a liberal Democratic president or candidate had acted in the ways Donald Trump has in his personal life, many of these evangelical leaders would be savaging that person based on the conviction that personal morality in political leaders matters. That is, after all, precisely what they did during the presidency of Bill Clinton.

Here is Gary Bauer, today a vocal Trump supporter but in 1998 the head of the Family Research Council: "The seamy facts under public discussion are shameful enough. But fascination with this story should not be allowed to obscure the deeper lesson these incidents impart. That lesson is this: Character counts—in a people, in the institutions of our society, and in our national leadership."[21] In the same year Franklin Graham wrote that Bill Clinton's affair with Monica Lewinsky should not just concern his family but "the rest of the world," adding, "If he will lie to or mislead his wife and daughter, those with whom he is most intimate, what will prevent him from doing the same to the American public?"[22]

Yet today, with Trump as president—when the excuse that failure to support Trump would lead to a Hillary Clinton presidency is long gone—many evangelical leaders dismiss those concerns almost entirely, some even invoking the Bible as their *defense* for Trump's outrageous conduct. They are, in fact, using many of the same arguments used by Clinton's defenders in the 1990s to respond to criticisms by the religious Right.[23]

A set of data points illustrates the double standard we're seeing. In October 2016—several weeks after the release of the notorious *Access Hollywood* tape in which Trump bragged about his affairs and declared that when you're a star, "You can do anything. Grab them by the pussy. You can do anything"—more than seven in ten (72 percent) white evangelical Protestants said an elected official can behave ethically even if they have committed transgressions in their personal life. Five years earlier, when Barack Obama was president, only 30 percent of white evangelical Protestants said the same. No group shifted their position more dramatically than white evangelical Protestants.[24]

But it's not only Mr. Trump's sexual transgressions that are relevant here; it's the whole package deal. Mr. Trump lies pathologically. He exhibits crude and cruel behavior, relishes humiliating those over whom he has power, and dehumanizes his political opponents, women, and the weak. He is indifferent to objective truth, trades in conspiracy theories, and exploits the darker impulses of the public. His style of politics is characterized by stoking anger and grievances rather than demonstrating empathy and justice. In sum, Mr. Trump embodies a Nietzschean morality rather than a Christian one. It is a repudiation of Christian concern for the poor and the weak, instead offering disdain for the powerless. Donald Trump's perspective is might makes right.

To be clear, Trump's most visible and vocal Christian supporters aren't responsible for the character flaws and ethical failures of the president. But by their refusal to confront those flaws and failures, they are complicit in the debasement of American culture and politics. Even more personally painful to me, they are presenting a warped and disfigured view of Christianity to the world. They are effectively blessing a leader who has acted in ways that are fundamentally incompatible with a Christian ethic.

A friend of mine who is an atheist told me that what is unfolding is "consistent with what sociobiology theorizes about religion: its evolutionary purpose is to foster in-group solidarity. Principles serve rather than rule that mission." This certainly isn't my view of faith, but in the current circumstances—given what is playing out in public—this is not an unreasonable conclusion for him to draw. And he's not alone. This kind of perception is multiplying. The evangelicals I have mentioned are doing more to damage the Christian witness than the so-called New Atheists ever could.

It's hardly a surprise that in 2018 confidence in the church or organized religion dropped from the previous year, from 41 percent to 38 percent. According to Gallup, "This is another all-time low for an institution whose highly positive image has been shrinking since its peak 68% great deal/quite a lot confidence rating in 1975. The church had been the top rated institution in the 1973–1985 surveys."[25]

FEAR AMONG THE FAITHFUL

So how did we get to this present place?

How on earth did we end up in a situation where, in the words of Redeemer Presbyterian Church's Tim Keller, one of the most trusted evangelicals in the world, "'evangelical' used to denote people who claimed the high moral ground; now, in popular usage, the word is nearly synonymous with 'hypocrite'"?[26]

It's a long and complicated story.[27] Part of the answer is undoubtedly that some evangelicals are giving in to the ancient temptation of being too close to political power, choosing to be court pastors to win the favor of the king. They are thrilled to be taken seriously, thrilled to be invited to the White House, thrilled to be seen as having influence in the highest ranks of political power.

That's understandable; motivations are always mixed and never entirely pure, and pride often rears its ugly head in situations like this. Rather than acknowledge this, however, what we're often getting is a spiritual show, a Christian Potemkin village, with people self-sacralizing their ambitions. (I know one person, a conservative commentator, who has justified his reluctance to publicly criticize President Trump because, he told me, he believes doing so will destroy his ability to witness to him.)

A more benign interpretation, as I understand the position of certain Christian leaders, is that access to power and influence has positive policy ramifications. I've stayed up until 3:00 a.m. talking with close friends—people of integrity with good hearts—who are aggrieved by my public criticisms of President Trump. In their defense of Trump's evangelical supporters they argue that it is essential to influence the administration on issues that matter to politically conservative Christians. (They have in mind court appointments and pro-life policies, in particular.)

That position has a certain logic to it, but it comes with a price. Because of Trump's narcissism, anything less than a full-throated public defense of him is viewed as disloyal. So to maintain their influence and access, many evangelical leaders have offered up outlandish rationalizations for the president. Faith becomes something to be used instrumentally, something to be publicly compromised in order to have a seat at the table of the politically powerful. And it raises the question, Where do evangelicals draw the line? At what point do they say that access to power isn't worth debasing themselves and their faith? The answer with Trump—at least so far, at least for many of the most politically prominent evangelicals—is never.

"Once you have made the world an end, and faith a means, you have almost won your man, and it makes very little difference what kind of worldly end he is pursuing," C. S. Lewis wrote in *The Screwtape Letters*, in which a senior devil offers advice to a junior devil. "Provided that meetings, pamphlets, policies, movements, causes, and crusades matter more to him than prayer and sacraments and charity, he is ours."[28]

Another explanation for what is unfolding within American Christianity is political tribalism, which is hardly a new phenomenon but is more acute than in the past. There is intense partisan loyalty at play—a feeling of belonging and community, a sense of shared purposes and shared adversaries, an eagerness to have political views reaffirmed and celebrated, and the belief that the enemy of my enemy is my friend.

The result is that faith is subordinated to partisanship rather than partisanship being diluted by faith. When you become part of a team, including a political team, it can blind you to alternative perspectives and facts. In many cases political affiliations, not theological truths, are given priority. Politics is the lens through which reality is interpreted, the mold in which attitudes and sensibilities are formed.

"Political homogeneity in the evangelical world is unhelpful to America," James Forsyth, a close friend who was born in Scotland and is now the senior pastor of the church my family and I attend in McLean, Virginia, said to me. Many evangelicals also feel increasingly powerless, beaten down, aggrieved, and under attack—and in some cases, they are. The elite culture is hostile to some traditional Christian beliefs.

The massive cultural shifts we have seen, especially in the realm of human sexuality, have left them with a sense that they've gone from being a "moral majority" to a persecuted minority. A sense of ressentiment, or a "narrative of injury," is leading some evangelicals to look for scapegoats to explain their growing impotence. People filled with anger and grievances are easily exploited. "Christians and people on the right start by believing they are fighting satanic forces," a person who is generally quite sympathetic to Christians told me, "and in the process become nihilists." It is as if there's a deep emotional need for a dark narrative.

Part of the explanation has to do with worry bordering on panic, including fear of lost status and influence. "We used to be the home team," one theologian told me. "Now we're the away team."

The fear is that the America many white evangelicals knew and cherished is fading away; that the United States is in a moral freefall; that our problems are overwhelming and almost beyond our capacity to fix them.[29] "We are on the verge of losing America" is a common refrain one hears. One pastor told me that Christians he interacts with "speak about losing their country with an intensity as if they are losing their God."

What Americans therefore need, many evangelicals believe, is an alpha male, a strongman, a person who will hit back against his critics (and their critics) ten times harder than they were hit. The Baptist pastor of a Dallas-based megachurch, Robert Jeffress, says Trump's tone doesn't bother him because "I want the meanest, toughest SOB I can find to protect this nation."[30] Liberty University president Jerry Falwell Jr., in a tweet, declared this: "Conservatives & Christians need to stop electing 'nice guys.' They might make great Christian leaders but the US needs street fighters like @realDonaldTrump at every level of government b/c the liberal fascists Dems are playing for keeps & many [Republican] leaders are a bunch of wimps!"[31] And according to Tony Perkins of the Family Research Council, evangelicals "were tired of being kicked around by Barack Obama and his leftists. And I think they are finally glad that there's somebody on the playground that is willing to punch the bully."[32] That "street fighter," that "meanest, toughest SOB," that "somebody," is Donald J. Trump.

Although bully worship, as Orwell called it, is never justified, one must confess that there is a nub of a fair challenge in this claim. Religious conservatives may understandably ask a version of this question: "In a country where not all play by Marquess of Queensberry rules, where the stakes of politics are literally life and death—with hundreds of thousands of babies being aborted each year—and where Christianity and conservative values face real perils, how can we push back if we don't embrace some pretty rough hombres?"

There is, however, a better way.

THE RIGHT WAY OUT AND THE RIGHT WAY UP

Having worked in politics my entire adult life, including on presidential campaigns and in the White House, I understand that governing involves complicated choices, transactional dealings, and prudential judgments. No one ever gets things exactly right, and all who choose to serve deserve our prayers for wisdom. Politics is certainly not a place for the pursuit of utopia and moral perfection; rather, at its best, it is about achieving the best approximation of the public good, about protecting human dignity and advancing, even imperfectly, a more just social order.

But with political involvement come temptations and traps, and it is the responsibility of Christians to act in ways that maintain the integrity of their public witness and improve our politics. The fact that this isn't happening is what makes this moment so troubling.

I am not a prophet, nor am I a theologian or church leader. Still, based on my experience and based on my extensive conversations with such leaders and with others dedicated to living out their faith with integrity in the political sphere, I would point to four aspirations Christians should strive for if they wish to redeem this moment:

1. That Christians begin with Jesus, tying their efforts to what he actually taught and modeled.
2. That Christians, especially evangelicals, articulate a coherent vision of politics, informed by their moral vision of justice and the common good.
3. That Christians model and maintain a deep attitudinal shift away from a spirit of anger toward understanding, from revenge toward reconciliation, from grievance toward gratitude, and from fear toward trust and love.
4. That Christians treat all types of people as "neighbors" they are to love.

1. Begin with Jesus

Christians need to reacquaint themselves with the Jesus of the New Testament, not the Jesus of the right-wing media complex. The real Jesus demonstrated a profound mistrust of political power, declined Satan's offer of the kingdoms of the world and their glory, and did not encourage his disciples to become involved in political movements of any kind.

The most meaningful emblem of Christianity is not the sword but the cross, which is the antithesis of worldly power. Unlike Muhammad, Jesus made it clear time and again that his kingdom is not of this world. And the New Testament, which offers detailed thoughts on all sorts of matters—from the qualifications for being an elder to parenting advice to how women should adorn themselves—does not provide anything like a governing blueprint.

The early church did not hand out voter guides. What it *did* do, according to the sociologist of religion Rodney Stark, is create "communal compassion" and social networks; care for the sick, widows, and orphans; welcome strangers and care for outsiders; respect women; and connect to non-Christians. That is how a tiny and obscure messianic movement in the second and third centuries became the dominant faith of Western civilization. That is how it transformed the ancient world and the course of human history.

To repeat: this does not mean that Christians, Christian institutions, and churches should never under any circumstances be involved in politics, since politics has profound human consequences. What it *does* mean is that Christians need to take on a much different posture than many of them have, to move away from hyperpartisanship toward a more detached and prophetic role, and to take more seriously than many do the idea of dual citizenship—the belief that we are citizens of the City of Man but that our deepest loyalties are to the City of God. This ought to create some safe distance from the principalities and powers of this world.

A proper political theology would prevent Christians, Christian institutions, and churches from becoming pawns in political power games. That may sound so obvious as to be banal, but evangelical Christians in particular—not all, but many—have been as susceptible to manipulation as any group involved in politics that I've seen.

"The church must be reminded that it is not the master or the servant of the state, but rather the conscience of the state," Martin Luther King Jr. said. "It must be the guide and the critic of the state, and never its tool."[33] Today, far too many evangelical Christians—however admirable they may otherwise be and despite the many good works they may do—are tools of the Republican Party and the Trump presidency.

2. Articulate a Coherent Vision

Evangelicals need to develop a theory of political and social engagement that is far more comprehensive and careful, mature and informed, textured and sophisticated. Too often our political aspirations have been defined by the moment or by others and so seem to change and shift according to who is pulling the strings.

In this respect, evangelicals and Protestants have much to learn from Catholicism, which has laid out and built on principles of social teaching over many centuries, often through encyclicals like Leo XIII's *Rerum Novarum* (Of the new things), which addressed the condition of the working class, and John Paul II's *Centesimus Annus* (The hundredth year), which expounded on issues of economic and social justice at the time of the collapse of Soviet Communism and reflected on the political, economic, and moral components of a free society.

The cornerstones of Catholic social thought are human dignity; subsidiarity, which holds that nothing should be done by larger and more complex institutions that can be done as well by smaller and simpler ones; and solidarity, meaning the social obligations we have to one another, with a special concern for the poor and most vulnerable members of the human community.

(Many of us who are non-Catholic but have had great respect for the teachings of the Catholic Church have been shaken to our core by the sickening and shameful sexual abuse scandals, by the Church's efforts at cover-ups, and by the failure to prevent further abuse.)

As Michael Gerson puts it when describing Catholic social thought, "The doctrinal whole that requires a broad, consistent view of justice, which—when it is faithfully applied—cuts across the categories and clichés of American politics. Of course, American Catholics routinely ignore Catholic social thought. But at least they have it. Evangelicals lack a similar tradition of their own to disregard."[34]

Unless and until some similar approach begins to take hold— and is transmitted from theologians and church leaders to the wider community of believers—the random, ad hoc nature of evangelical political involvement will continue and probably worsen. There is no authoritative theological construct in place to check, channel, and refine raw partisanship cloaked in Christian garb.

3. Model a Deep Attitudinal Shift, Biased Toward Unity

A third thing that needs to happen is in some senses the most fundamental, which is a deep attitudinal shift among many politically active Christians—to move away from a spirit of anger toward understanding, from revenge toward reconciliation, from grievance toward gratitude, and from fear toward trust. Fear is prevalent, but for Christians, love casts out fear.

Ken Stern is a fair-minded liberal who spent a year with people on the right to better understand their worldview. (His book,

Republican Like Me: How I Left the Liberal Bubble and Learned to Love the Right, documents his journey.) Stern visited evangelicals in a variety of settings and was impressed by the generosity he encountered. A pastor friend and I met with him for lunch. Here are the questions Stern posed to us: Why, since so many evangelicals live lives devoted to helping others, does that not translate into a political agenda that reflects that fact? How is it that the "culture war" issues succeed in becoming the public face of Christianity, while the many acts of kindness and charity, and the spirit informing those things, are kept under a bushel, largely out of public view? Why consistently show your worst side rather than your most winsome one?

We wondered the same thing.

It's been said that C. S. Lewis and J. R. R. Tolkien never lost their wonder and enchantment with the world. It's an unfortunate commentary on the state of things that the same can be said of so few public, and certainly so few politically active, evangelicals.

In his book *What's So Amazing About Grace?* Philip Yancey tells of how prior to writing his book he began asking a question of strangers when striking up a conversation. "When I say the words 'evangelical Christian' what comes to mind?" Yancey wrote that he mostly heard *political* descriptions—and not once did he hear a description redolent of grace.

Yancey adds this:

> Grace comes free of charge to people who do not deserve it
> and I am one of those people. I think back to who I was—
> resentful, wound tight with anger, a single hardened link in a
> long chain of ungrace learned from family and church. Now
> I am trying in my own small way to pipe the tune of grace.

I do so because I know, more surely than I know anything, that any pang of healing or forgiveness or goodness I have ever felt comes solely from the grace of God. I yearn for the church to become a nourishing culture of that grace.[35]

It's true enough that a common error within Christianity is to use grace as a way to elide wrongdoing, and that those who are willing to stand up for biblical morality can easily (and unfairly) be caricatured as ungracious. But Yancey's insights are worth considering in the context of Christians and their role in and impact on public matters. He's a faithful follower of Jesus who sees things from a perspective that is not only biblically grounded but desperately needed because it's in such short supply.

4. Become Loving Neighbors

Which leads me to the fourth thing Christians can do to strengthen our public witness and the state of our politics: internalize and act on the lessons from an ancient parable. The one I have in mind is Jesus's parable of the Good Samaritan, and it speaks to this moment in a powerful way.

The context of the story is that Jesus, who declared that we should love our neighbor, is asked, "Who is our neighbor?" The parable—found in the tenth chapter of the Gospel of Luke—is Jesus's response.

In the story, a Samaritan comes across a Jew who has been beaten, robbed, and left dying on the side of a dangerous road from Jerusalem to Jericho. After a priest and Levite both ignore the wounded man, the Samaritan rescues him and, at his own expense, nurses him back to health. "Go and do likewise," Jesus says.

What makes this parable so extraordinary and relevant to us is that there was deep enmity between Samaritans and Jews at the time; they despised each other. They had practically no dealings with each other. It was the first-century version of political, ethnic, and religious tribalism, with the Samaritans in particular marginalized, oppressed, and viewed with suspicion.

The point Jesus was driving home is that we need to break down the walls between us. We are called to love our "neighbors," which, according to the parable, are those who are racially, religiously, ethnically, and culturally different than we are, and to help them in their need in the most practical way, materially and physically.

All of this has obvious lessons for the here and now. Our politics is polarized and tribalized. Many Americans view "the Other"—for some, these are refugees, Muslims, and Mexicans; for others, it's rural southerners, gun owners, and religious fundamentalists—with suspicion and contempt. That combination of suspicion and contempt is eating away at our sense of national unity and runs counter to what Jesus taught.

Christians can model what it means to reach across the divides that exist in their work settings, in their churches, in their social circles, and in what they say on social media. They can demonstrate tolerance and understanding toward those with different life experiences. They can be intentional about putting themselves in volunteer settings that put them in contact with people who have different political views, skin color, national origins, and class status.

The way to create a bond between people isn't sitting across a table from each other talking about bonding; it's to put them in situations where they're working shoulder-to-shoulder in pursuit of a common goal, especially a humanitarian one.

There's no magic wand we can wave to repair the breach. A nation's civic and political culture is changed by what we do in our daily lives, in our homes, schools, communities, and houses of worship. And by loving our neighbors we take the most important first step. This is what Jesus calls his followers to do, and what citizenship in twenty-first-century America demands.

REDEMPTION AND RECONCILIATION

Five years ago, my friend Steve Hayner mentioned to me that he was going through the Gospel of Luke and was struck again with the grace and embrace Jesus extended to those whom the religious elite had every reason (they thought) to kick to the curb. People on the low rungs of life, including those with frailties and flaws, flocked to Jesus—not because he preached moral rectitude but because he was willing to love them, to listen to them, and to welcome them.

"I'm sure that many were self-justifying and hardened in their life patterns," Steve wrote me. But Jesus's main mission was to convince them of God's love and invitation. And then he went on to speak about those willing to stand in the middle of the tensions that necessarily attach to faithful living in a broken world.

"I doubt whether God will have much to say about our political convictions in the end," Steve said to me, "but I'm quite sure that he will have something to say about how we loved the least, the marginalized, the outcasts, the lonely, the abused—even when some think that they have it all. Political convictions that lead toward redemption and reconciliation are most likely headed in the right direction."

This isn't a prescription for a particular kind of political involvement. It's certainly not a road map on how to deal with complicated public issues. It is, however, a reflection on *how* Christians should engage the world, including the political world. There is great wisdom in his insights, and great richness in these words: *redemption* and *reconciliation*.

The successful political-social movement I have in mind will require Christians to make a compelling case for social order and moral excellence, but done with a generosity of spirit, all the while offering a healing touch, especially to those who are suffering and living in the shadows of society.

It will require Christians to be less fearful and more hopeful, less anxious and more confident that God is sovereign and his purposes don't ultimately rest on their efforts. Christians engaged in public life should model calm trust rather than panic and vitriol born of anxiety. We are called to be faithful, not successful; to act with integrity, not to become just another special interest group whose worth is measured by its influence on the politically powerful.

"All admirable," some of my Christian conservative friends may say, "but just words. Don't you know we're under siege by the radical Left and the hostile secular culture? Don't you realize that if we do not push back, now and hard, we may lose the very liberty to practice and embody the values you celebrate? What you say is fine for ordinary times, but these are desperate times that require desperate measures—such as Donald Trump."

I do hear, but I don't agree. First, because my friends' fears are simply not justified by facts. Second, because even if the times were desperate, responding with fear and anger and in ways that betray our own teaching will cloud our vision and sabotage our battle. Embracing Trump, whose defining characteristics include dishonesty and exploitation, does not help us. Third, because by letting fear rule, we open ourselves to far too easy manipulation by fearmongers and demagogues, who are expert at scaring up our money and votes for their own profit and power. And fourth, because being political outsiders or even a cultural minority is not something to fear in the first place. Historically, Christianity has done its best work and exerted its greatest influence not from a position of political dominance but while being faithful even from a position of political weakness. For all those reasons, fear, as a basis for Christian politics, is our enemy, not our friend. It is not our weapon; rather it controls us and eventually can consume us.

"We need a gospel culture as opposed to a political culture," James Forsyth told me. "Jesus challenges all our categories— political, theological, ethnic, racial, cultural." He added, "What we need is a humble remapping of cultural engagement."

How will that occur? Admonitions offered in good faith may help here and there. In the end, though, it will require a transformation of individual hearts, a reordering of priorities. It will require from people of faith more modesty and less rigid, off-putting certainty. It will require seeing the virtues in our opponents and the shortcomings in our allies and ourselves. And it will require people of faith to see the world through gentler eyes. That isn't likely to happen unless some inner transformation happens. It has occurred before. "Do not be conformed to this world, but be transformed by the renewing of your mind, so that you may prove what the will of God is, that which is good and acceptable and perfect," the Apostle Paul wrote in his letter to the Romans.[36]

History has shown that politics can be a more noble enterprise when it is twinned with faith, but only faith properly understood and properly executed. It turns out that this is a good deal easier to get wrong and a good deal harder to get right than I once thought.

I'm not willing to give up on this linkage, this alliance, at least not yet. But to my coreligionists I would say this: we need to do it right and we need to do it a whole lot better, for the sake of American politics, for the sake of a more just social order, and for the sake of our Christian witness to an increasingly skeptical and jaded world. I may not be certain how we can accomplish what many of us aspire to, but I am confident I know how God and the world will judge whether we are doing it in a way that deserves the label "Christian."

CHAPTER 5

Why Words Matter

uzzallo Library is the main, majestic library located on the campus of the University of Washington, where I attended college. From time to time on Friday and Saturday evenings, when my friends were busy with social activities, I would ensconce myself there, not to focus on homework assignments but rather to listen to speeches by John F. Kennedy.

I did so often enough that I eventually memorized different JFK speeches—a few in whole, most of them in part: his inaugural address and the one accepting the Democratic nomination in 1960, his "Ich bin ein Berliner" remarks in West Berlin, and the "peace address" at American University, his civil rights address to the nation, and the "We choose to go to the moon" speech at Rice University, his farewell address to the Massachusetts legislature, and more.

I did this despite the fact that I was a Republican, having cast my first vote for Ronald Reagan in 1980. That is less incongruous than it may seem if you take into account that Kennedy was a Democrat when Democrats were much more conservative than today. (On some issues Kennedy ran to Nixon's right during their presidential contest, including hammering then Vice President Nixon for the "missile gap" between the United States and the Soviet Union, which in fact did not exist.)

But what appealed to me most was not Kennedy's political profile. I was certainly taken in part by the elegance and grace, the charm and high culture that characterized the Kennedy presidency. "The Kennedys lit up the White House with writers, artists, and intellectuals," according to the historian Alan Brinkley, "the famous cellist Pablo Casals, the poet Robert Frost, the French intellectual André Malraux."[1]

But I was primarily caught up in the power and beauty of Kennedy's words, which captured my imagination and further persuaded me that politics can be a high calling.[2] In those years the thing I wanted to be most of all was an advisor to the president who, in one way or another, used words in the service of the nation.

Two decades later, I was deputy director of presidential speechwriting for George W. Bush during and after September 11, 2001, a moment when presidential words were particularly important—in expressing collective grief and sorrow, in channeling the public's fear and rage, in creating national unity and tamping down bigotry against Muslims, in explaining to the American people an enemy almost all of them were unfamiliar with (al Qaeda), and in summoning the nation to war.

The words of a president always matter, but in this case they *really* mattered. All of a sudden the days of the little-noticed Lincoln Day dinner speech, remarks at a steelworkers picnic, or the National Future Farmers of America speech seemed trivial. When the president addressed a joint session of Congress nine days after the attacks, it galvanized the nation. National Hockey League games were halted so players and fans could watch the speech on a video screen. One colleague said it was "a nearly universal American experience." There was a sense that President Bush's words were not just for the moment but for history.[3]

THE POWER OF WORDS

Democracy requires that we honor the culture of words. Modern democracies arose as a correction to absolute monarchies and the long human history of "might makes right." The very idea of democracy is based on the hope that fellow citizens can reason together and find a system for adjudicating differences and solving problems—all of which assumes there is a shared commitment to the integrity of our public words. When words are weaponized and used merely to paint all political opponents as inherently evil, stupid, and weak, then democracy's foundations are put in peril.

Words have extraordinary power. Think for a moment how moved you are by the lyrics of your favorite song, by your favorite books and poems, by a letter from a loved one. Words are the means by which we convey our deep emotions and longings, knowledge and understanding, hopes and fears. We use them to teach, to warn, to inspire, to defend truth, to seek justice.

"My task which I am trying to achieve is, by the power of the written word, to make you hear, to make you feel—it is, before all, to make you *see!*" This is how the novelist Joseph Conrad defined his mission as a writer. "That—and no more: and it is everything! If I succeed, you shall find there according to your deserts: encouragement, consolation, fear, charm—all you demand; and, perhaps, also that glimpse of truth for which you have forgotten to ask."[4]

The use of words by novelists and politicians is not identical, but the very best politicians use words in some of the same ways novelists like Conrad did—to make us hear, to make us feel, to make us see.

My belief, which is undoubtedly influenced by my history as a speechwriter, is that we need to understand much better than we do the role of words in the mission of politics. We need to know why using words as weapons against others and against truth is a travesty. We need to recognize why our political culture allowed for the rise to power of Donald Trump, a mendacious propagandist. And we need to offer ideas on what our institutions and we as individuals can do about it.

Words have long been a treasured part of American political history. It's telling that when Americans call to mind their greatest presidents, they often think of them not so much for their policies as for their words.

We think of Thomas Jefferson less as the person who pulled off one of history's most consequential land deals, the Louisiana Purchase, from which fifteen states, in part or in toto, were eventually created. Instead we recognize him primarily as the man who wrote the Declaration of Independence and authored the phrase "All men are created equal."

We think of Abraham Lincoln less for the Homestead Act, which opened government-owned land to small family farmers, than for his second inaugural—"With malice toward none, with charity for all"—and the Gettysburg Address: "Four score and seven years ago our fathers brought forth on this continent, a new nation, conceived in Liberty, and dedicated to the proposition that all men are created equal."

We think of Franklin Roosevelt less for the Lend-Lease Act, which helped Great Britain and our other allies survive the Nazi offensive, than for saying, "We have nothing to fear but fear itself" and declaring that December 7, 1941, when Japan attacked Pearl Harbor, was "a date which will live in infamy."

John Kennedy is remembered less for his handling of the Cuban missile crisis than for a single line in his inaugural address: "Ask not what your country can do for you; ask what you can do for your country." And many fewer people know the specifics of Ronald Reagan's 1981 tax cuts and 1986 tax reform, which were huge legislative achievements, than know his line "Mr. Gorbachev, tear down this wall."

Rhetoric, then, has an important place in the hearts of men and women, as well as in America's political and social history. Words can articulate and set out national goals, express national resolve, promote healing and understanding, educate the public and explain complicated issues, galvanize a nation behind great causes, and rally a nation in times of war. It was said of Churchill, during the dark days and darker nights when England was under Nazi attack, that he "mobilized the English language and sent it into battle."[5]

The same was true of Thomas Paine, the English-born Enlightenment figure who was a pivotal political theorist and polemicist on behalf of the American Revolution. Paine argued against the British monarchy and for American independence; to that end he produced the most widely read and influential pamphlet of the American Revolution, *Common Sense*. Paine gave public voice to many private beliefs and galvanized populist and elite opinion in America. He gave words to the case for American independence without which it really might not have happened. And he did so by reaching higher, by connecting events to principles and ideals. John Adams said, "Without the pen of the author of *Common Sense*, the sword of Washington would have been raised in vain."[6]

Words can also stir within the hearts of people anger at unrighteousness. Frederick Douglass achieved this during his extraordinary July 5, 1852, speech, which included a searing indictment of America. "What, to the American slave, is your 4th of July?" Douglass asked. "I answer; a day that reveals to him, more than all other days in the year, the gross injustice and cruelty to which he is the constant victim. . . . There is not a nation on the earth guilty of practices more shocking and bloody than are the people of the United States, at this very hour."

A very different approach to indicting a nation's wrongdoing and shaping its moral sensibilities can be found in Harriet Beecher Stowe's *Uncle Tom's Cabin*, one of the most affecting and influential novels in American history. Upon meeting Stowe, Abraham Lincoln reportedly said to her, "Is this the little woman who made this great war?" One Southerner said the 1852 novel "had given birth to a horror against slavery in the Northern mind which all the politicians could never have created."[7]

David S. Reynolds's book *Mightier Than the Sword* analyzes the enormous impact of *Uncle Tom's Cabin* and shows how it broadened and deepened the public's revulsion at slavery. The abolitionist William Lloyd Garrison was known for his acidic rhetoric and denunciations of those whom he considered to be insufficiently antislavery. The Constitution, Garrison said, was "a covenant with death and an agreement with hell."[8] Harriet's brother Henry believed Garrison was well intentioned but lacking in "conciliation, good-natured benevolence, even a certain popular mirthfulness." According to Henry, "Anti-slavery under [Garrison] was all teeth and claw. . . . It fought. It gained not one step by kindness. . . . It bombarded everything it met, and stormed every place which it won."[9]

Harriet Beecher Stowe took things in a different direction. According to Reynolds:

> The novel's relatively benign treatment of Southerners was deliberate. Because Stowe wanted the South to change its mind about slavery, she avoided the kind of wholesale demonization of slaveholders she feared might alienate all Southerners. She actually had two Southern characters, Emily Shelby and St. Clare, speak *against* slavery. By doing so, she felt she could challenge the South's peculiar institution from within by having some slave owners say that slavery was evil.[10]

Reynolds adds, "In fact, her efforts to be compassionate made her seem far *more* dangerous than virulent abolitionists like Garrison, whose rancorous tone and calls for disunion made him easily dismissable in the South and unpopular even in the North."[11]

Stowe herself wrote to a friend a year and a half after the publication of *Uncle Tom's Cabin*, saying,

> The effects of the book so far have been, I think, these: 1st. to soften and moderate the bitterness of feeling in *extreme abolitionists*. 2nd. to convert to abolitionist views many whom the same bitterness had repelled. 3rd. to inspire the free colored people with self-respect, hope, and confidence. 4th. to inspire universally through the country a kindlier feeling toward the negro race.[12]

Stowe's genius, then, wasn't simply in the realm of imaginative literature; it was also in moving America in the direction of justice.

She achieved that not through abstract demands but through direct appeals to decency and compassion. She humanized slavery through vivid, memorable figures both heroic (Uncle Tom) and sadistic (Simon Legree). She understood the power of grace in the pursuit of a principled cause. And she knew that at its best and deepest level, politics has to be understood as part of a great human drama. That is the way one shapes, in a lasting way, public sentiment and moral beliefs. And that is something only a very few political leaders today grasp.

Uncle Tom's Cabin was "doing a magnificent work on the public mind," one journalist at the time said. "Wherever it goes, prejudice is disarmed, opposition is removed, and the hearts of all are touched with a new and strange feeling, to which they before were strangers."[13]

This is the force and impact words can have on the soul of a nation. Words are not simply descriptive; they can be *aspirational*. But even more than that, words can help us better understand ourselves. They bind us together. In politics they articulate for us what goals we are trying to reach, so that it is more than just a struggle for power. We reach higher truths through words.

TRUMP'S WAR ON THE CULTURE OF WORDS

But words can just as easily be *misused*—and so become instruments not for healing but for division, not to enlighten but to deceive, not to educate but to indoctrinate. If you believe words can ennoble, you must also believe they can debase. If they can elevate the human spirit, they can also pull it down. Which brings us back once again to the dismal, demoralizing Trump era.

It is certainly true that plenty of politicians have pulled the human spirit down over the years. We've not exactly been living through a golden age of political rhetoric. There is not a Demosthenes among us. But in America today we have arrived at a low moment when it comes to the quality of words and political rhetoric. That's true pretty much across the board; among state legislators and governors, in the House and Senate, there are no great orators, countless mediocre ones, and a few downright awful ones.

But the debasement of words has reached a zenith with the coming of America's forty-fifth president. In America it is the president who sets the tone for the nation, who has far and away the largest megaphone, and who creates the example, the template, that others follow.

President Trump dominates discourse in this country in ways no other president ever has. His mastery of social media—and the media's ravenous need to cover Trump's every utterance—has given him the ability to invade and permeate people's thoughts and lives in unique ways. Before we can hope to repair the damage, we need to understand what it is—*precisely what it is*—about Trump's misuse of words that is so pernicious and dangerous.

The indictment starts with the sheer banality of his words. During his presidency, Donald Trump has uttered no beautiful and memorable phrases. His inaugural address, which is a speech normally meant to inspire the citizenry, is remembered, if at all, for the phrase "American carnage" and Trump's description of a dystopian nation, broken and shattered. In almost every case his use of words reflects his attitude toward politics: transactional, unreflective, amoral, emotive, stripped of nobility and high purpose.

More worrisome is that Trump's extemporaneous answers are often an incoherent word salad. Confused answers often—

not always, as in the case of Dwight Eisenhower, but often—represent a confusion of thought, and that's certainly the case with President Trump.

If you read the transcripts of many of his interviews and extemporaneous speeches, you will find what millions of Americans witnessed during his debates during the 2016 campaign: Donald Trump is not only often unable to lay out a coherent argument; at times he's unable to string together sentences that parse. One illustration is the speech Trump gave in South Carolina during the 2016 campaign:

> Look, having nuclear—my uncle was a great professor and scientist and engineer, Dr. John Trump at MIT; good genes, very good genes, OK, very smart, the Wharton School of Finance, very good, very smart—you know, if you're a conservative Republican, if I were a liberal, if, like, OK, if I ran as a liberal Democrat, they would say I'm one of the smartest people anywhere in the world—it's true!—but when you're a conservative Republican they try—oh, do they do a number—that's why I always start off: Went to Wharton, was a good student, went there, went there, did this, built a fortune—you know I have to give my like credentials all the time, because we're a little disadvantaged—but you look at the nuclear deal, the thing that really bothers me—it would have been so easy, and it's not as important as these lives are—nuclear is so powerful; my uncle explained that to me many, many years ago, the power and that was thirty-five years ago; he would explain the power of what's going to happen and he was right—who would have thought? But when you look at what's going on with the four prisoners—

now it used to be three, now it's four—but when it was three and even now, I would have said it's all in the messenger; fellas, and it is fellas because, you know, they don't, they haven't figured that the women are smarter right now than the men, so, you know, it's gonna take them about another 150 years—but the Persians are great negotiators, the Iranians are great negotiators, so, and they, they just killed, they just killed us.[14]

Finding other examples is simply too easy. He speaks like this most every day.

During his run for the presidency, Trump admitted that he didn't prepare for debates or study briefing books, and it showed. (He believed such things got in the way of a good performance.) He said judges sign bills. (They don't.) He confused the Kurds, a large ethnic group in the Middle East, and the Quds Force, a special forces unit of Iran's Revolutionary Guard. He offered contradictory views on the minimum wage (wages are too high and then too low; he was for it and then against; he favored enforcement by the federal government and then wanted states to take the lead). On abortion, he argued that women who have abortions should be "punished" even as he praised Planned Parenthood, the largest abortion provider in the country. He wasn't aware of Vladimir Putin's aggressions against Ukraine until ABC's George Stephanopoulos pointed it out to him. In an interview with CBS's Scott Pelley, Trump claimed in one sentence that taxes on the wealthy would be raised and in the next agreed that Republicans don't raise taxes. He claimed his administration would deport 11 to 12 million illegal immigrants, but that "we're rounding 'em up in a very humane way, a very nice way."

He has been no better on this front as president. On illegal immigration, he promised to remove "really bad dudes" in the country through the use of a "military operation," forcing his then secretary of homeland security to declare, "There will be no use of military forces in immigration. None." At a press conference with Israeli prime minister Benjamin Netanyahu, he declared his ambivalence about a two-state solution between the Israelis and the Palestinians, forcing his UN ambassador to correct the statement. He declared NATO "obsolete" and threatened that the United States would not fulfill key elements of its obligations, forcing his secretary of defense to reaffirm our support for NATO. The president declared he "absolutely" believes waterboarding is an effective interrogation technique, forcing his CIA director to state that the agency would "absolutely not" bring back waterboarding as an enhanced interrogation technique.

Things got so bad that during the 2018 Munich Security Conference, and amid global anxiety about President Trump's approach to world affairs, US officials communicated a message to a gathering of Europe's foreign policy elite: "Pay no attention to the man tweeting behind the curtain."[15]

Early in his term, Trump gave an interview in which he said his administration would quickly put out its own health proposal, which would cover everyone now insured and cost much less. One problem: there was no Trump proposal at the time. It was the creation of his own imagination. Republicans on Capitol Hill and Mr. Trump's own team were utterly perplexed by what Mr. Trump said.

The president wrongly stated that stock market gains are helping to pay down the national debt. During a meeting in the Roosevelt Room he embraced a Democratic plan, with no provisions attached, to provide amnesty to undocumented immigrants who came to the US as children—before then House majority leader Kevin McCarthy was forced to intervene and explain to the president that he did not support the plan just embraced. And Trump wasn't aware that the Social Security Disability Insurance program is part of Social Security.

No president has ever been quite as disdainful of knowledge, as indifferent to facts, as untroubled by his benightedness. And through his words, the president is not only spreading ignorance; he is glorifying it.

At the same time as he enjoys winging it in terms of American policies, on some matters he uses words strategically and with forethought. When it comes to dealing with those who oppose him, he consistently uses words to demean, belittle, bully, and dehumanize.

He has described his adversaries as "crazy," "psycho," a "maniac," a "monster," and a "nut job." He refers to the press as "the enemy of the people." He mocked a *New York Times* journalist with a physical disability, ridiculed Senator John McCain for being a POW, made a reference to "blood" intended to degrade a female journalist (Megyn Kelly), and compared one of his Republican opponents to a child molester. He linked Ted Cruz's father to the assassination of JFK and suggested that a former White House advisor to Bill Clinton, Vince Foster, had been murdered (despite five separate investigations that found this claim to be utterly false). As president he insulted MSNBC's Mika Brzezinski, calling her "crazy" and accusing her of "bleeding badly from a facelift" (just one in a long list of instances where Trump ridiculed women based on appearance). He has attacked gold star parents and widows.

The number of targets is inexhaustible because Trump's brutishness is inexhaustible. America's most visible public figure possesses a streak of cruelty that he won't control, which he promiscuously and proudly displays, and which is amplified by social media. But Trump's attacks aren't simply directed toward individuals he is upset with and dislikes. He also uses words to divide America along racial and ethnic fault lines.

It's hardly a coincidence that Mr. Trump burst onto the national political scene in 2011 by claiming that Barack Obama, our first black president, was not a natural-born American citizen but rather was born in Kenya. (He later implied that Obama was a secret Muslim and dubbed him the "founder of ISIS.") And since the first day he stepped onto the presidential stage, he has stoked grievances, resentments, and fear of the Other, including Mexicans, Muslims, and Syrian refugees.

Mr. Trump engaged in a racially tinged attack on Gonzalo Curiel, a district court judge presiding over a fraud lawsuit against Trump University, calling Curiel a "hater" who was being unfair to him because the judge is "Hispanic," because he is "Mexican," and because Trump said he would build a wall on the southern border. (Judge Curiel was born in Indiana.) Trump also expressed doubt that a Muslim judge could remain neutral in the case. As president, Trump claimed "some very fine people" were marching in a Charlottesville, Virginia, march that included neo-Nazis and white supremacists, an event that turned violent and led to the death of a young woman. He has attacked the intelligence of black athletes (LeBron James), black journalists (Don Lemon and Abby Phillip), and black members of Congress (Maxine Waters), and referred to his former White House advisor and reality television colleague Omarosa Manigault Newman, who is black, as a "crazed, crying lowlife" and a "dog."

This is not the conservatism of the British statesman Edmund Burke and the political philosopher Michael Oakeshott or former vice presidential candidate Jack Kemp and President Ronald Reagan. It is blood-and-soil conservatism primarily aimed at alienated white voters who believe they have lost the country they once knew. No president in living memory, no major political figure since George Wallace, has said things that stir the hearts of white supremacists as Donald Trump does. (It is hardly an accident that David Duke has repeatedly praised Trump.)

Past presidents have had varying degrees of success when it comes to uniting the nation, and at times their words and actions have exacerbated our divides. And of course being a polarizing figure is not a problem per se. Many of the most impressive and consequential individuals in American history—Lincoln, FDR, Martin Luther King Jr., and Reagan—were viewed as divisive figures. The difference is that Trump takes great delight in provoking acrimony, malice, and bitterness *for their own sake*; in turning Americans against each other *in order* to turn them against each other. As one source close to the Trump White House told Axios's Mike Allen, the president, in order to stir up his base, looks for "unexpected cultural flashpoints."[16]

One example: in September 2017, after Trump was criticized by some of his base for being too sympathetic to children of illegal immigrants who had been brought to America, he went to Huntsville, Alabama, and gave a speech for a senate candidate, Luther Strange. What was notable about the speech isn't that Trump praised Strange but that Trump weighed in, apropos of nothing, on the issue of NFL players not kneeling for the national anthem in order to protest incidents of police brutality. (Seventy percent of NFL players are black.) "Wouldn't you love to see one of these NFL owners, when somebody disrespects our flag, to say, 'Get that son of a bitch off the field right now. Out. He's fired. He's fired,'" Trump said.[17]

The previous week only a handful of players—a half dozen—had refused to stand for the national anthem, and it had no policy implications. Yet Trump weighed in, knowing his words would both reconnect him to his base and provoke a passionate, emotional response and catalyze a racially charged debate that would further rend American society. (The week after Trump attacked NFL players, in a show of defiance, hundreds of them refused to stand for the national anthem, a response Trump had to be thrilled by.)

What we have, then, is a president who, in ways we have never quite seen before, uses words to divide and embitter, to appeal to our basest and ugliest instincts. The effect is like throwing grains of sand into the eyes of others: it causes aggravation, irritation, and pain, and can damage delicate tissue. The only way to stop the damaging effects is to remove the sand from the eyes.

KILLING TRUTH

The banality and weaponization of Trump's words are bad enough, but perhaps the greatest cause for concern is his nonstop, dawn-to-midnight assault on facts, on truth, on reality. That places Trump in a sinister category all his own.

You often hear from Trump supporters that all politicians lie, and Trump is no worse than the rest. But that is nothing but a clumsy effort to defend a man who is habitually dishonest.

Here's the reality: many politicians are guilty of not telling the full truth about events. A significant number shade the truth from time to time. A few fall into the category of consistent, outright liars. But only very few—and only the most dangerous ones—are committed to destroying the very idea of truth itself. That is what we have in Donald Trump, along with many of his top aides and courtiers. And it started in the opening hours of his presidency.

During an appearance on NBC's *Meet the Press* shortly after Donald Trump took office, host Chuck Todd asked White House counselor Kellyanne Conway why the White House had sent Press Secretary Sean Spicer to the briefing podium to falsely claim that "this was the largest audience to ever witness an inauguration, period."

"You're saying it's a falsehood. And they're giving—Sean Spicer, our press secretary—gave alternative facts," she said. To which Todd responded, "Alternative facts aren't facts, they are falsehoods."

Later in the interview, Todd pressed Conway again on why the White House sent Spicer out to make false claims about crowd size, asking: "What was the motive to have this ridiculous litigation of crowd size?"

"Your job is not to call things ridiculous that are said by our press secretary and our president. That's not your job," Conway said.

Todd followed up: "Can you please answer the question? Why did he do this? You have not answered it—it's only one question."

Conway said: "I'll answer it this way: Think about what you just said to your viewers. That's why we feel compelled to go out and clear the air and put alternative facts out there."[18]

In one sense, of course, Spicer's lie, which was done at the behest of Trump, was trivial. Did it really matter if Obama had a larger crowd at his inauguration than Trump did? Who cares? But in another sense, the lie was significant because *it was a lie about a demonstrable fact.*

It was a lie everyone knew was a lie.

There was photographic evidence that Obama's inaugural crowd was much larger than Trump's. What Trump instinctively understood was the disorienting effect this type of lie, compounded by countless other lies, has on people. It overwhelms the brain, which can't process all the false information. The result is that we tire of counteracting every lie and begin to absorb some of them. And Conway, in saying that the White House felt "compelled" to put out "alternative facts," was giving the green light to Trump supporters to construct their own reality. They were off to the races, and how: Sean Spicer's successor as press secretary, Sarah Huckabee Sanders, sent out on Twitter a doctored video produced by an editor at the conspiracy website Infowars intended to show CNN's Jim Acosta inappropriately placing his hands on a White House intern during a contentious press conference. This qualifies as the textbook definition of propaganda, and it perfectly fit with the Trump presidency. (The White House revoked Acosta's press pass but it was later restored by a federal judge.)

After 773 days in office, Trump made more than 9,000 false or misleading claims, which averages out to more than 11 per day.[19] In 2018, Trump averaged 15 false claims a day.[20] (In the 7 weeks before the 2018 midterm elections, he averaged nearly 30 a day.)[21] That is a staggering, unprecedented achievement.

The sheer scope, breadth, and shamelessness of the Trump lies are impressive in their own corrupt way. Mr. Trump told falsehoods about voter fraud costing him the popular vote to Hillary

Clinton (it didn't), Russian intervention in the 2016 election being a hoax (it wasn't), having won the biggest landslide since 1980 (not even close), and President Obama bugging Trump Tower (it never happened). He prevaricated in claiming his 2018 State of the Union was the most watched of any State of the Union in history, in stating that tax reform cost him a fortune, and in claiming credit for business investments and job announcements that had been previously announced. He was wrong when he asserted that he had signed more bills than any president ever, that counterprotesters in Charlottesville didn't have a permit, and that the *New York Times* had apologized for "bad coverage." Trump claimed the FBI inspector general's report on Hillary Clinton's email server totally exonerated him; it did no such thing. He claimed that the policy of separating migrant children from their parents was forced on him by Democrats; the person responsible for the policy was Trump, not Democrats.

For two years President Trump, his legal team, and his advisors denied that he was involved in hush money payments to Stormy Daniels and Karen McDougal; we now know that was a lie and Mr. Trump was involved in or briefed on every step of the agreements. On dozens of occasions since the summer of 2016 Mr. Trump said he had "nothing to do with Russia"—no deals, no investments, no business with Russia. Those claims were lies.

Mr. Trump claimed he had never heard of WikiLeaks when news stories about it came out in 2016; in fact, he had spoken about it years earlier. In November 2018, he claimed that "I don't know Matt Whitaker," whom he had named to be acting attorney general after he asked Jeff Sessions to resign; the previous month, in an interview with *Fox & Friends*, Trump had said, "I know Matt Whitaker." Mr. Trump claimed the Paris Agreement on climate change was binding; it's not. In 2018 he claimed, "We don't have tariffs anywhere"; that year the US had placed levies on more than $300 billion in imports. He asserted that America had trade deficits with nearly every country; we have a trade surplus with more than one hundred nations.

The president said thousands of people had been brought in on buses from Massachusetts to vote illegally in New Hampshire; there's no evidence that occurred. Trump told a group of sheriffs that the murder rate in the United States was the highest it's been in "forty-five to forty-seven years"; in reality, it has dropped to rates we have not seen since the 1960s. He claimed people in California were rioting over sanctuary cities; no such thing happened. The president claimed that a large migrant caravan moving toward the Mexican-US border included "unknown Middle Easterners" mixed in; there was no evidence to support that assertion. On and on it goes. On a single day, the president publicly made 125 false or misleading statements in a period of time that totaled only about 120 minutes.[22]

My own experience might provide some useful context here. I recall how, as a White House speechwriter, I was pressed by the staff secretary to prove any conceivably questionable claim. If I raised even the slightest dissent—this claim is self-evident and therefore doesn't have to be sourced, that claim is too small a matter to worry about—she would say to me and to others, in a tone that conveyed a kind of deep civic conviction, "If the president says it, it needs to be correct." Now, we certainly got things wrong, as have other administrations. But the mistakes weren't intentional, and if we discovered them, we tried to correct the record.

What is notable about the Trump presidency are the number

and velocity of the falsehoods and misleading statements. They have been made in speeches and tweets, on matters significant and trivial, about others and about himself—and he virtually never apologizes or issues corrections. He says what he wants, when he wants, regardless of the reality of things.

"The man lies all the time," according to Thomas Wells, Trump's former lawyer.[23] Tony Schwartz, the cowriter of *The Art of the Deal*, says that "lying is second nature to him."[24] In Bob Woodward's book *Fear*, Trump's former personal lawyer John Dowd describes the president as "a f****** liar," telling Trump he would end up in an "orange jump suit"[25] if he testified to special counsel Robert Mueller.[26] And former White House aide Anthony Scaramucci, when asked during the CNN interview if he considers Trump a liar, admitted, "Okay, well we both know that he's telling lies. So if you want me to say he's a liar, I'm happy to say he's a liar."[27] (In a later interview Scaramucci put it this way: "He's an intentional liar. It's very different from just being a liar-liar.")[28]

Trump is not simply a serial liar; he is attempting to murder the very idea of truth, which is even worse. Without truth, a free society cannot operate. Which is why Trump's rhetoric ought to matter to all of us, and why it is our civic duty to call out his lies in every way we can.

THE POST-TRUTH MOMENT

That Donald Trump is a con man is beyond dispute.[29] Why he became one is an interesting and important psychological question. But an even more urgent one is how our political culture allowed him to win the Republican nomination and the presidency.

The answer, at least in part, is that polarization and partisanship have reached a toxic level. For a large number of Americans, truth is viewed as instrumental, a means to an end. Everything is liable to become a weapon in our intense political war. And getting to this "post-truth" political moment was a good deal easier than one might imagine.

Some new research regarding confirmation and disconfirmation bias may help us understand how we got here. Confirmation bias is the tendency to interpret new evidence as confirmation of one's existing beliefs and the tendency to reject new evidence that challenges one's existing beliefs.

They are perennial human problems, and there are understandable reasons why, starting with the physiological component. Jack Gorman, a psychiatrist, and his daughter Sara, a public-health specialist, have explored this matter in their book *Denying to the Grave: Why We Ignore the Acts That Will Save Us*. They cite research suggesting that processing information which supports our beliefs leads to a dopamine rush, which creates feelings of pleasure. "It feels good to 'stick to our guns' even if we are wrong," the Gormans told Elizabeth Kolbert in the *New Yorker*.[30] The moral psychologist Jonathan Haidt, author of *The Righteous Mind*, says that "extreme partisanship may be literally addictive."[31]

On the flip side, "When something is inconsistent with existing beliefs, people tend to stumble. . . . [I]nformation that is inconsistent with one's beliefs produces a negative affective response," according to Norbert Schwarz, Eryn Newman, and William Leach, experts in cognitive psychology.[32]

Brian Resnick reports that researchers at New York University's brain-imaging center are exploring how our brains are hardwired for partisanship and how that skews our perceptions in public life. Once a partisanship mentality kicks in, according to Resnick, the brain almost automatically prefilters facts—even noncontroversial ones—that offend our political sensibilities.

"Once you trip this wire, this trigger, this cue, that you are a part of 'us-versus-them,' it's almost like the whole brain becomes re-coordinated in how it views people," says Jay Van Bavel, the leader of NYU's Social Perception and Evaluation Lab.[33]

Our beliefs are also often tied up with our identities. "If changing your belief means changing your identity, it comes at the risk of rejection from the community of people with whom you share that identity," according to Dr. Christine Herman.[34] That is difficult for any of us to do, and it explains why we tend to reject facts that may challenge our identity- and group-determining beliefs.

Dan Kahan, a psychology professor at Yale University, points out that fans of opposing teams tend to see different things when there's a close call by officials.[35] It's not that fans who react one way are faking their reaction while others are authentic; it's that they actually perceive things differently.

In a sense, we see what we want to see in order to believe what we want to believe. In addition, we all like to be proven right, and changing our views is an admission that we were previously wrong, or at least had an incomplete understanding of an issue.

There is also an enormous amount of information to process in the world; we often need categories and ways of thinking and like-minded individuals to help us sort out information. None of us has the time or inclination to closely examine the validity of the endless amount of information coming our way.

For example, what are the best studies on gun control and what do they show us? Do proposed gun control laws work where they have been tried? If so, how well? If easy access to guns makes deadly violence more common—and that is certainly an understandable concern given that gun death rates in the United States dwarf every other developed country in the world—how reasonable is it to expect that we can extinguish the supply of guns in America, which is approaching 300 million? How applicable are, say, the Australian and British examples to ours? Are their models—Australia and Britain have enacted some of the strictest gun control laws in the world after mass shootings[36]—ones for us to follow?

What about the data on the role guns play in self-defense? And what about the argument that killers often choose no-gun zones (like schools and movie theaters) to commit gun violence? This is a lot to sort through on just this one topic, so we often rely on authority figures in a given field, deferring to their judgments and expertise. And we almost always ascribe greater authority to those whose worldview we share.

As a species, then, we are ever in search of data that confirms what we want to believe, what we already believe. "L'illusion est le premier plaisir" (Illusion is the first of all pleasures), Voltaire said. We are all tempted by delusions and denials so long as they constitute bricks in the walls we have chosen to build and to live behind. We are also profoundly incurious when it comes to thinking in different ways about things on which we have strong beliefs. Our inclination to do this is particularly strong in times of division and dispute, when we seem to lack reliable authority figures in various fields. And we are plainly living in such a moment now.

So why is confirmation bias having a more harmful effect today than it has in the past? A big part of the reason is that because of demographic shifts and communication technologies, we are more likely today to live in a bubble than in the past. We live with—and we get our information from—people who think like we do.

As we have already established, our nation is increasingly polarized and fragmented. Our capacity to hear one another and reason together has become deeply impaired. Facts are seen by many people as subjective and malleable, so we lack a shared context to talk about our problems. As a result, more and more Americans are effectively living in a self-created political reality. It's now possible to isolate oneself in an information space that entirely confirms one's preexisting views and biases.

Normal confirmation bias is now on steroids, and some are exploiting this situation for profit and so further exasperating the problem. An influential Republican lawmaker admitted to me that some of those in the right-wing media complex have made a successful business model by defacing facts to fit the worldview of the hosts. His point was that it wasn't simply a case of dealing with true believers; there's a financial incentive to distort the truth.

In 2016, Oxford Dictionaries declared *post-truth* as the word of the year. It refers to circumstances in which "objective facts are less influential in shaping public opinion than appeals to emotion and personal belief." Oxford Dictionaries' president Casper Grathwohl said *post-truth* could become "one of the defining words of our time."[37]

The great scholar and senator Daniel Patrick Moynihan said decades ago, "Everyone is entitled to his own opinion, but not to his own facts." No one disputed Moynihan's point. But on November 30, 2016, during an interview on the *Diane Rehm Show*, Trump supporter and then CNN contributor Scottie Nell Hughes said this:

> Well, I think it's also an idea of an opinion. And that's—on one hand, I hear half the media saying that these are lies. But on the other half, there are many people that go, "No,

it's true." And so one thing that has been interesting this entire campaign season to watch, is that people that say facts are facts—they're not really facts. Everybody has a way—it's kind of like looking at ratings, or looking at a glass of half-full water. Everybody has a way of interpreting them to be the truth, or not truth. There's no such thing, unfortunately, anymore as facts.

And so Mr. Trump's tweet [sic], amongst a certain crowd—a large part of the population—are truth. When he says that millions of people illegally voted, he has some—amongst him and his supporters, and people believe they have facts to back that up. Those that do not like Mr. Trump, they say that those are lies and that there are no facts to back it up.[38]

This has been a narrative pushed by Mr. Trump and his top advisors, including his top legal advisors, during his presidency. In a July 25, 2018, speech to a Veterans of Foreign Wars convention, President Trump said, "And just remember: What you're seeing and what you're reading is not what's happening."[39] In other words, who are you going to believe—me or your lyin' eyes?

A month later, the president's lawyer, Rudy Giuliani, asserted during an interview with NBC's Chuck Todd over the Mueller investigation, "Truth isn't truth."[40] Another of the president's lawyers, Jay Sekulow, when called out for making a false claim to defend Mr. Trump, replied, "Facts develop."[41]

Comments such as these might be excused as mere slips of the tongue, if not for the fact that the president and all the president's men and all the president's women act as if truth were merely subjective, utterly pliable, and completely in the eyes of the beholder.

The modus operandi of Trump World is this: If facts exist that are incriminating to Mr. Trump, dismiss the facts. Label them fake news. And go on lying.

Journey back with me to the 1970s. When Richard Nixon's "smoking gun" tape was released in 1974, revealing an effort to get the CIA to intervene with the FBI to stop the Watergate investigation, no one denied the reality and meaning of the tapes. Nixon knew he would have to resign; his supporters had no way to defend him. The empirical ground on which they stood had crumbled. The facts were the facts, and they were indisputable. Yet if the same thing were to happen today—if tapes were released proving Donald Trump had committed an unlawful and impeachable act—some large number of the president's supporters would reject the tapes as the product of "fake news." Trump's unrelenting battering of the press has discredited it so much in the eyes of many of his supporters that they will reject any and all criticisms of Trump, regardless of the merits.

The television critic for the *New York Times*, James Poniewozik, says the goal of the president is to argue that "there is no truth, so you should just follow your gut & your tribe."[42]

"This is the conversation the White House wants," according to the Associated Press's Jonathan Lemire. "Make everything muddy so partisans gravitate to their own corners."[43]

Nietzsche coined a term, *perspectivism*, to describe the idea that there is no objective truth, everybody gets to make up their own reality, their own script, their own set of facts, and everything is conditioned to what one's own perspective is.

Here's an illustration of what this looks like in practice. During a segment on CNN, former Speaker of the House Newt Gingrich, one of Trump's most prominent advocates, defended

Trump's false claim that crime rates were soaring, insisting the average American "does not think crime is down, does not think they are safer."

When the host, Alisyn Camerota, cited FBI data to support her claim that we are safer and crime is down, Gingrich was unimpressed. He responded, "No. That's your view." When Camerota countered that this wasn't simply a subjective matter and once again cited FBI crime statistics, Gingrich responded, "As a political candidate, I'll go with how people feel, and I'll let you go with the theoreticians."[44] In other words, facts be damned; my feelings will create my own reality.

On a large enough scale, this kind of attitude stands to yield epistemological anarchy; that is, there are no knowable truths to appeal to. When *that* happens, we're bargaining for a lot of trouble. How does a democracy function if there are no shared facts?

A combination of factors—social media and new technology platforms; micro-targeting and psychometric methods in political campaigns; unprecedented polarization and hyperpartisanship; the fragmentation of traditional media sources and the advent of information silos; and the intervention in our elections by hostile powers using "fake news," misinformation, and disinformation—has reshaped American politics. The capacity to inject poison into our political bloodstream—in the form of lies and falsehoods, crazed conspiracy theories, smears, and dehumanizing attacks—is unprecedented. And there are very few authority figures or institutions, inside politics or outside, that can provide an antidote to the poison.

The reason is that we live in an age of deep distrust, with Americans' confidence in the nation's major institutions having dropped to a historic low point.[45] Only one in ten Americans say they have a great deal or quite a lot of confidence in Congress, highlighting what Gallup has called "the nation's most important problem: a dysfunctional government that has lost much of its legitimacy in the eyes of the people it serves."[46]

Americans, then, remain reluctant to put much faith in most of the institutions at the core of American society. What this means is that there are far fewer institutions and figures of authority who can declare certain things to be outside the boundaries of responsible discourse and be listened to; who can say that certain claims are preposterous and should be ignored. Instead, people who make false, outrageous, and even indecent assertions are finding validation, affirmation, and quite a large audience.

Take as an example the radio host Alex Jones, who runs the fake news website Infowars.com. Jones is a conspiracy monger who has alleged that the US government allowed the 9/11 attacks to happen and who claimed the Sandy Hook massacre was a hoax.

When pressed in an interview with journalist Megyn Kelly about the Sandy Hook massacre, Jones said, "I tend to believe that children probably did die there. But then you look at all the other evidence on the other side. I can see how other people believe that nobody died there." But as Ms. Kelly pointed out, "There is no evidence on the other side."[47]

Nevertheless, according to Kelly, Jones's YouTube monthly views reached 83 million in November 2016, more than five times higher than the previous November; Infowars.com got a temporary White House press pass for the first time; and Donald Trump, who was interviewed by Jones in December 2015, called him after the election to thank him for his help.

As recently as a decade ago Alex Jones would have been viewed as a crank on the fringes of American political life, with very little influence. But in the Trump era he has been legitimized in the eyes of many. To them, he's a trusted voice, a source of information and confirmation. As alluded to earlier in this chapter, the White House press secretary sent out a doctored video by an editor at Infowars to justify revoking the press pass for a CNN White House correspondent.

To be sure, there is a continuum; some propagandists are worse than others. But the combined effects are deeply damaging. "The point of modern propaganda isn't only to misinform or push an agenda," according to the Russian dissident and former world chess champion Garry Kasparov. "It is to exhaust your critical thinking, to annihilate truth."[48]

In the new media ecosystem, then, everything is up for grabs. We often don't have a common set of facts we're working from. In the past our differences were generally over solutions, meaning different views on the best approaches and policies to address the problems we face. Today there are differences in epistemology, the theory of knowledge that allows us to distinguish facts and justified belief from opinion. As a result, people are increasingly living in their own realities, creating their own facts, writing their own scripts. Facts are to be molded like Play-Doh.

I want to be clear: it's not as though most Americans consider politics to be a fact-free zone, and most people would undoubtedly find Alex Jones's influence on our political and civic culture to be harmful. The concern, though, is that a minority of reckless, nihilistic voices—who have the ability to garner much attention and cause much disruption—are poisoning our political culture. Their influence is disproportionate to their numbers and is threatening to kill American politics.

It may be helpful to think of it like the concept of herd immunity. So long as a certain percentage of the population is immune from infection, the healthy herd provides protection to those who are not, since spread of the contagious disease is contained to an isolated few. But if a society drops below a threshold—say, 85 percent—herd immunity is lost. The disease spreads to the herd. And those who were protected no longer are.

There can also be seepage. While the most outlandish conspiracies might not be believed, a general, corrosive distrust can spread. People begin to view as optional facts that in the past would have been accepted. It's as if consumers of information are walking through a cafeteria, choosing the facts they like and walking past the ones they don't. Again, this kind of thing has been present throughout much of our history. What's different now is how widespread this phenomenon is.

LIVING IN TWO UNIVERSES

We are losing a common factual basis for our national life.

In 2009 Rush Limbaugh, easily the most influential figure in the history of conservative talk radio and one of the dominant figures in conservatism over the last quarter century, devoted part of his show to what those on the right referred to as "Climategate," a hacking scandal involving the release of more than one thousand emails among scientists at the Climate Research Unit of the UK's University of East Anglia. Those who deny global warming claimed (wrongly) that the emails proved the fabrication of the global warming crisis.[49] Limbaugh referred to the institutions of government, academia, science, and media as the "four corners of deceit." And he went on to say this:

We live in two universes. One universe is a lie. One universe is an entire lie. Everything run, dominated, and controlled by the left here and around the world is a lie. The other universe is where we are, and that's where reality reigns supreme and we deal with it. And seldom do these two universes ever overlap.[50]

David Roberts of Vox.com writes:

In Limbaugh's view, the core institutions and norms of American democracy have been irredeemably corrupted by an alien enemy. Their claims to transpartisan authority—authority that applies equally to all political factions and parties—are fraudulent. There are no transpartisan authorities; there is only zero-sum competition between tribes, the left and right. Two universes.[51]

I don't think Limbaugh would dispute that characterization, and in fact the intensity of his feelings has only increased in the intervening years. But here's the point: if you believe conservatives and liberals live in two universes, one of which is a pack of lies while in the other reality reigns supreme, then compromise is impossible. Even argument becomes impossible since there are no shared facts and assumptions on which persuasion is possible. To compromise would be treasonous. Political opponents are enemies.

Take as one example the aftermath of the 2018 school shooting in Parkland, Florida, in which seventeen people (primarily high school students) were massacred. In the past, tragedies such as this would have united people in grief and sympathy. No more. The charges leveled by each side against the other were instantaneous and incendiary. The left was saying that the right loves guns more than their children; the right was saying the left hates guns more than it loves their children. Each was accusing the other of being willing to sacrifice the lives of their children on the altar of their pro- and anti-gun ideology. This political impasse is belied by the fact that most polls indicate that the vast majority of Americans are worried about how to protect their children from gun violence.

In such a toxic and mistrustful environment—partisan antipathy is at a record level, according to the Pew Research Center[52]—it's hard to reason together. Debate becomes much more difficult. And when we lose the ability to persuade, all that's left is compulsion and the exercise of raw power, intimidation, and silencing those with whom we disagree.

We are becoming a country without shared facts or reference points. Yale Law professor Stephen L. Carter puts it this way:

> When disputes over facts are misconstrued as disputes over principles, the entire project of Enlightenment democracy is at risk. The liberalism of the Enlightenment rested critically on the supposition that agreement on the facts was a separate process from agreement on the values to be applied to them. The social theorist Karl Mannheim, in "Ideology and Utopia," argued that we would never be able to separate the two, that we would always wind up seeing the facts through the lens of our preformed ideologies. Thus liberal democracy, in the Enlightenment sense, was bound to fail.[53]

Our challenge is to prove Mannheim wrong, and right now we're not doing as well as we should at that.

WHAT WE CAN DO

Everyone, including journalists, has a role to play if we are going to recover from this "post-truth" political moment. For our news channels, that starts, but hardly ends, with showing more ideological balance as a way to rebuild trust with Red America. (Only 11 percent of Republicans consider information from national news organizations to be very trustworthy, according to a 2017 Pew Research Center poll.)[54]

In one study, half of the journalists surveyed identified themselves as independents. But among journalists who align with one of the two major parties, four in five said they're Democrats.[55] Tom Rosenstiel, executive director of the American Press Institute, says, "The best data out there shows that there are fewer Republicans working in traditional newsrooms and news generally than there used to be."[56]

The common rejoinder of journalists is that while as individuals they may be liberal, that does not influence their coverage. But the liberalism manifests itself in subtle and not-so-subtle ways, from story selection to tone and intonation to the line of questioning that's pursued. Rosenstiel acknowledges that the imbalance "affects the discussion in newsrooms even when people are trying to be fair."

The result is that many people on the right have felt unheard, their views disrespected and delegitimized. In an effort to find an outlet, conservatives turned to alternative sources of information, from talk radio to the Fox News Channel to right-leaning websites. That was understandable, and in some respects it was healthy, offering a greater diversity in viewpoints than there once was. There was an imbalance and a need for correction.

But something happened along the way. People who in the past viewed news outlets as *biased* now view them as *fraudulent*. That's an unfair judgment, and yet we need to recognize that the attitude exists, it arose from a very real bias, and so long as that attitude continues, there's little hope we can agree on a set of shared facts.

This is only part of the task, though. Both journalists and news consumers also need to take it upon themselves to push back against rushing a story or wanting to sensationalize it. Journalists need to resist breathless reporting, jumping to premature conclusions, and galloping ahead of the facts. What we need, in a phrase, is self-restraint. The more ferocious the attacks made against the press, the more detached and dispassionate, fair-minded, and even-handed the press needs to become. As a friend has put it to me, "As things speed up, we need to slow down." So, too, the American media.

Maggie Haberman, an influential reporter for the *New York Times*, did her part to slow things down last year. After nine years, 187,000 tweets, and building up a list of close to 700,000 Twitter followers, she wrote a column announcing she was stepping away from Twitter. It was distorting discourse, she said, and she couldn't turn off the noise.

"The viciousness, toxic partisan anger, intellectual dishonesty, motive-questioning and sexism are at all-time highs," Haberman wrote, "with no end in sight." She added, "Twitter is now an anger video game for many users. It is the only platform on which people feel free to say things they'd never say to someone's face. For me, it had become an enormous and pointless drain on my time and mental energy."[57] (She has since returned to Twitter, as have other journalists who temporarily forswore it.)

Journalists also need to do less advocacy, to show less eagerness for stories to come out a certain way, to not allow adrenaline rushes to drive reporting. "Our facts need to be squeaky clean and uncorrupted," CNN's Jake Tapper said in a speech to the Los Angeles Press Club. "We are not the resistance, we are not the opposition, and we are here to tell the truth and report the facts regardless of whom those facts might benefit. . . . [L]et us be revolutionaries by telling the truth at this time of deceit. But let us also make sure that we get our facts right."[58]

Corporations need to do due diligence when it comes to the sites they are advertising on, to ensure that hateful and bigoted ones aren't inadvertently being supported. And when it comes to misinformation/disinformation campaigns that are being coordinated by hostile regimes like Russia, we need to learn from countries like Ukraine, which has experienced this and is beginning to take steps to defend itself.

One example of this is Stopfake.org, whose goal is to verify and refute disinformation and propaganda about events in Ukraine being circulated in the media and which now examines and analyzes all aspects of Kremlin propaganda, including in other countries and regions.[59] "But perhaps the most important component of our effort," former secretary of state Madeleine Albright has said,

> is to try to help foster constructive engagement between government, civil society, and technology firms. These companies have an interest in working with us on solutions, because disinformation is hurting their platforms and making them less usable. We cannot expect the technology companies to fight back on their own, but they cannot

expect those of us working in civil society or government to solve the problem without their help. So we need the technology community to acknowledge the problem and be open to partnership.[60]

There are structural solutions to look at, then—practical steps to help us repair our civic and political damage. But something else, something deeper, must change as well: citizens need to renew their commitment to truth itself and be willing to fight for it and to fight falsity.

"Facts inform opinions, and opinions, inspired by different interests and passions, can differ widely and still be legitimate as long as they respect factual truth," wrote the political theorist Hannah Arendt. She added, "Freedom of opinion is a farce unless factual information is guaranteed and the facts themselves are not in dispute. In other words, factual truth informs political thought just as rational truth informs philosophical speculation."[61]

Destroy the foundation of factual truth, and lies will be normalized. This is what the Czech dissident (and later president) Václav Havel described in the late 1970s when he wrote about his fellow citizens making their own inner peace with a regime built on hypocrisy and falsehoods. They were "living within the lie." In such a situation life becomes farcical, demoralizing, a theater of the absurd. It is soul destroying.

The United States is still quite a long way from the situation Havel found himself in. But to keep it that way—to keep civic vandalism from spreading—we all have a role to play. The first thing is to refuse to become complicit in the lies, to refuse to believe them and certainly to not spread them, including lies that may help your political causes. Call out the most damaging lies—to friends, in social settings, on social media. Be civil, but be forceful. Name it. If enough people do, it actually can start a movement.

One suggestion: start a discussion thread on Facebook or Twitter and tag your representative on it. Make it clear that when the president engages in a sustained attack on the truth, you expect your representative to speak out against it, and in some cases take specific actions to hold him accountable. It may be voting for censure, it may be insisting that Congress hold hearings on a matter in dispute, and it may be going on record that if the president impedes or kills a truth-seeking legal investigation then there will be a hellacious price to pay, from blocking all nominations and legislation to impeachment. It is a truism in politics: the way to make those in public office see the light is for them to feel the heat.

Fatalism is never an option in a self-governing republic, and it's a particularly bad attitude these days. Utilize the means that are available to you to influence your elected leaders. The best way to influence a member of Congress is to visit their office. Writing a letter to them or a letter to the editor tends to be more effective than a phone call. Better yet, show up at town hall meetings and public events. If you have financially supported a party that is aiding and abetting a compulsive liar, end the support—and give the reason why. Help create a constituency for new leadership that prizes integrity and esteems honor. This may strike you as being as realistic as Locke's castle in the air. It's not. People who have a corrupting influence have been voted into office; they can be voted out of office.

Beyond that, as citizens we can reject party loyalties when they are at odds with truth. As important as our political parties are to the health of our nation, they are not more important than truth itself or to the ideals of governance both parties were built on. That is why we must refuse to support candidates who are chronically dishonest. In doing so, we are rejecting a corrosive approach to politics. One person acting alone may not make much of a difference. A lot of people acting together create a culture.

There are other things that can be done as well, including not getting all your information from the same partisan sources every day. Diversify your reading and news habits. Become discriminating customers of information. Cultivate critical reasoning skills. And remind yourself that the point of gathering information isn't necessarily to reaffirm the views you already hold; it's to gather information in order to better ascertain the truth. Try to interact with people who have a different political perspective than you do—and when you do, listen to understand, not just to refute.

These are concrete steps that can be taken, but much of what needs to be done is in the realm of attitudes. As Havel put it,

> in its most original and broadest sense, living within the truth covers a vast territory whose outer limits are vague and difficult to map, a territory full of modest expressions of human volition, the vast majority of which will remain anonymous and whose political impact will probably never be felt or described any more concretely than simply as part of a social climate or mood. Most of these expressions remain elementary revolts against manipulation: you simply straighten your backbone and live in greater dignity as an individual.[62]

Straightening our backbones and living with greater dignity as individuals—a day at a time, an act at a time—is sound advice when it comes to repairing the damage America has sustained.

WORDS AS INSTRUMENTS OF PERSUASION AND REASON

"Politics and the English Language" was published in 1946 in the journal *Horizon* and is perhaps George Orwell's most famous and enduring essay. In it, he argues that the English language has become disfigured and degraded, "ugly and inaccurate because our thoughts are foolish, but the slovenliness of our language makes it easier for us to have foolish thoughts." Language, particularly political language, is not just a manifestation of our decline but also an instrument in it.

The important thing to understand is that what Orwell is aiming for is *clarity*. He wants language to be an instrument to express rather than conceal or prevent thought, and he's quite right about that.

Orwell's thoughts on *political* language merit particular attention. "In our time," he wrote, "political speech and writing are largely the defense of the indefensible." Political language consists largely of "euphemism, question-begging and sheer cloudy vagueness." He added, "Political language—and with variations this is true of all political parties, from Conservatives to Anarchists—is designed to make lies sound truthful and murder respectable, and to give an appearance of solidity to pure wind."

One senses in Orwell his frustration with the state of political speech because it often degrades what he considered precious, language; because it warped reality and the true nature of things; and because he understood the enormously high stakes in politics. If we get our politics wrong, Orwell knew, it can lead to misery and suffering, to gulags and concentration camps. "Every line of serious work that I have written since 1936 has been written directly or indirectly *against* totalitarianism," he said, "and *for* Democratic Socialism as I understand it."

Orwell believed political language matters because politics matter, that the corruption of one leads to the corruption of the other. He believed language was a means to see the truth and to tell the truth. He believed, too, in a moral code, in concepts like justice and objective truth. "The Party told you to reject the evidence of your eyes and ears. It was their final, most essential command," Orwell wrote in *1984*.

[Winston Smith's] heart sank as he thought of the enormous power arrayed against him, the ease with which any Party intellectual would overthrow him in debate, the subtle arguments which he would not be able to understand, much less answer. And yet he was in the right! They were wrong and he was right. The obvious, the silly, and the true had got to be defended. Truisms are true, hold on to that! The solid world exists, its laws do not change. Stones are hard, water is wet, objects unsupported fall towards the earth's center. With the feeling that he was speaking to O'Brien, and also that he was setting forth an important axiom, he wrote: *Freedom is the freedom to say that two plus two make four. If that is granted, all else follows.*[63]

The challenge of our time is to rediscover our best ends and noblest purposes. We can't give up on the belief that human beings are rational and reasonable, that evidence and logic matter, and that persuasion is possible. The human condition is such that things are rarely all of one and none of the other, and certainly in this case, the pendulum swings from moments of collective trust and calm reason to collective mistrust, emotivism, and rancor. In the world today there is pacific New Zealand on the one hand, and there is war-torn Syria on the other. In America there was the "era of good feeling" in 1815–25 and the Civil War in the 1860s, the placid 1950s and the raucous, angry late 1960s.

A lot of different factors—internal and external, domestic and international, economic and social—influence a nation's political and civic culture. And we all know, deep in our bones, that so does political leadership and rhetoric. We need to stand with men and women in public life who believe, as Lincoln did, that words can be instruments of reason and justice, repair and reconciliation, enlightenment and truth. Who are willing to challenge not just their adversaries but their allies, not just the other political tribe but their own. And who are willing to make a compelling case for deliberative democracy and persuasion.

"The posturing and pontificating we find in our messy public discourse are neighbors to a genuine democratic good—the practice of persuasion," writes Yale political science professor Bryan Garsten.

> In addressing our fellow citizens directly, we make an effort to influence them, not with force or threat or cries, but with articulated thoughts that appeal to their distinctly human capacity for judgment. In trying to persuade, we attend to their opinions without leaving behind our own, and so we try somehow to combine ruling and being ruled in the way

that democratic politics requires. While neither as powerful nor as ubiquitous as rhetoricians themselves might claim, persuasion is nevertheless a real possibility in democratic life, and it is a possibility that we ought to protect.[64]

Indeed it is, and indeed we should. We have to reclaim our language in order to reclaim our politics.

CHAPTER 6

In Praise of Moderation,
Compromise, and Civility

I n the 1990s I became a good friend of Joe Klein, who at the time was a columnist for *Newsweek*. Joe was more liberal than I, though we had similar instincts on several matters. We originally met, in fact, because of our interest in faith-based social programs. Our relationship was characterized by respect, affection, and interests beyond politics. He was delightful company.

Yet after I joined the Bush White House in 2001, our relationship hit a rough patch, particularly over the Iraq War. He believed I had gone over to the Dark Side; I felt that he was unfair and uncharitable in his critiques of President Bush and our administration. Neither of us was inclined to give ground; each of us was happy to point out the flaws we suddenly saw so clearly in each other.

Once I left the White House, our antipathy, rather than receding, went public. He wrote for publications attacking me; I was more than willing to write for publications attacking him. It got intense and personal. (A quick Google search will prove my point.) We were both inflamed because of our political differences.

During our estrangement, I justified my words and actions. "He was the aggressor," I told myself, "and when you're in the public arena you have to fight for what you believe and respond to those who attack you." I had people who agreed with me (and who disagreed with Joe) cheering me on.

But those who know me the best, like my wife Cindy, also knew that all along there was a part of me that felt like what was happening wasn't quite right—that this wasn't the way things ought to be—and eventually things would need to be repaired.

By the summer of 2015 I felt it was time to explore the possibility of reconnecting. It turned out it was. I reached out to Joe in an email, asking if a meeting was possible. He readily agreed, and we met for breakfast at the Jefferson Hotel in Washington, DC. Joe and I happened to see each other even before we entered the hotel and embraced on the street corner, almost before any words had been spoken between us. Reconciliation was now on track. Political differences had splintered our relationship; it was now being put back together. But it took time.

You may have experienced your own version of this. Differences with acquaintances and friends can quickly escalate; as a result, relationships can be strained and even reach the breaking point. Time and distance can help repair the breach. Passions cool, the gaps between you and the other person don't seem quite as wide. The qualities that once drew you to each other come back into focus. Conversations turn to topics deeper and more personal than politics.

But the restoration of fractured friendships isn't easy; it doesn't happen by accident, and politics can complicate things. That's especially true today, when our differences can seem so vast, and the feelings they stir up so fervent, that they overwhelm everything else. If we don't figure out a way to restrain these passions—and as this story attests, I find it as hard to achieve as you do—mutual contempt, incivility, and broken politics will be our fate.

NAVIGATING OUR WAY THROUGH OUR DIFFERENCES

As you look out at the broken state of our politics, lamenting its tone and shaking your head in disgust at the bickering and lack of cooperation, the mistake you're likely to make is the same one I can easily fall into: to assume that all would be right with the world if only more people agreed with me, if they saw things just as I see them, if they interpreted things just as I do—and if they don't, to get irritated at them for their ignorance and inflexibility, their flawed judgment and lack of self-awareness, for not sufficiently loving their country. To believe, in short, that they're not only wrong but deeply flawed as human beings.

Here's the thing, though: the people I'm quick to condemn because they hold different views than I do look at *me* the same way as I look at *them*. They believe that if only *I* thought more like *they* do, the acrimony and distasteful parts of politics would disappear.

In a sense, we're both right. It's true that if we only set aside our differences—if one side or the other jettisoned its beliefs in the name of agreement—our politics would be less acrimonious and gridlocked. But that hope is a fairy tale. To wish for it is to wish that pigs could fly.

The more pressing practical problem is not that we have differences, which always exist and will never entirely disappear. Rather, the problem is that we have lost the ability to navigate our way *through* our differences. In other words, the fact that we disagree on so much is not our main political and social challenge; the failure to find *reasonable accommodation* in the midst of those differences is.

The task of politics is to live peaceably with our differences and for people to find appropriate outlets for their views to be heard and represented. A healthy politics has as its goal not a civic nirvana where we all just get along, but a nation with enough sense of unity and common purpose to accept and overcome our differences—and where deep differences do exist, to debate them with words rather than fists or billy clubs or bullets, in ways that are characterized by intellectual rather than physical conflict.

Responsible citizenship means accepting that differences exist and will continue to exist. The urgent questions we need to wrestle with are these: What do we do about them? How do we live as one nation with deep differences, which aren't going away anytime soon? The answer: restore the democratic virtues that are necessary for a self-governing nation to thrive.

Before doing that, however, we have to ask ourselves the same question the American founders asked themselves: What is the proper way to understand human nature? The cure to what ails us depends on getting the diagnosis of the human condition right.

MEN ARE NOT ANGELS

At the core of every social, political, and economic system is a picture of human nature, to paraphrase the twentieth-century columnist Walter Lippmann. The presuppositions we begin with—the way in which the picture is developed—determines the lives we lead, the institutions we build, and the civilization we create. They are the foundation stone.

To simplify things a bit, within political philosophy over the last several centuries, there have been three main currents of thought about the nature of the human person. The first is that humans, while flawed, are perfectible. A second is that we are flawed and permanently so, and should accept and build our society around this rather unpleasant reality. A third view is that although human beings are flawed, we are capable of virtuous acts and self-government—that under the right circumstances, human nature can work to the advantage of the whole.

The first school included those who, representing the French Enlightenment, believed in the perfectibility of man and the pre-eminence of scientific rationalism. Their plans were grandiose, utopian, revolutionary, and aimed at "the universal regeneration of mankind" and the creation of a "New Man."

Such notions, espoused by Jean-Jacques Rousseau and other Enlightenment philosophes, heavily influenced a later generation of thinkers, including socialist theorists like Robert Owen, Charles Fourier, and Henri de Saint-Simon. They believed that human nature was easily reshaped. Human nature was considered plastic and malleable, to the point that there was no fixed nature to speak of; it could therefore be molded into anything the architects of a social system imagined.

The second current of thought, embodied in the writings of seventeenth-century Englishmen Thomas Hobbes (whom we met in chapter 3) and Bernard Mandeville, viewed human nature as more nearly the opposite: inelastic, brittle, and unalterable. And people were, at their core, antisocial beings.

Hobbes, for example, worried that people were ever in danger of lapsing into a precivilized state, "without a common power to keep them all in awe," which, in turn, would lead to a hopeless existence, a "state of nature" characterized by "a war of every man, against every man." To avoid this fate, we must submit to the authority of the state, which he termed the "Leviathan" (a monstrous, multiheaded sea creature mentioned in the Hebrew Bible). In the process, we would gain self-preservation, but it would come at the expense of liberty.

The third model of human nature is found in the thinking of the American founders. "If men were angels," wrote James Madison, the so-called father of the Constitution, in *Federalist Paper* No. 51, "no government would be necessary." But Madison and the other founders knew men were not and would never become angels.

They believed instead that human nature was mixed, a combination of virtue and vice, nobility and corruption. People are swayed by both reason and passion, capable of self-government but not to be trusted with absolute power. The founders' assumption was that within every human heart, let alone among different individuals, were competing and sometimes contradictory moral impulses and currents. ("Truly man is a marvelously vain, diverse and undulating object. It is hard to found any constant and uniform judgment on him," is how the French philosopher Michel de Montaigne put it.)

Here's the important point: the American founders believed we needed to create institutions that take into account aspects of human nature—"unfriendly passions," our tendency to factionalize, and our susceptibility to grievance and demagoguery—and constructively channel them; to "refine and enlarge the public view," in the words of *The Federalist*.

In particular, the founders accepted that deep differences were a given—their own experiences, including the Constitutional Convention in Philadelphia, underscored just how deep those differences could run—and wanted our political institutions to deal with them in ways that kept the republic from flying apart.

There are two methods of removing the causes of faction, according to Madison: "The one, by destroying the liberty which is essential to its existence; the other, by giving to every citizen the same opinions, the same passions, and the same interests."[1]

Since destroying liberty would be a catastrophe and it's impossible to give every citizen the same opinions, passions, and interests, factions were here to stay. (As a young boy, upon reading Montaigne, Madison wrote, "Our passions are like Torrents which may be diverted, but not obstructed."[2]) Our Madisonian system of government—based on checks and balances and separation of powers—was designed to push people toward accommodation. But what's happening right now is that it is pushing people toward *alienation*.

REBALANCING OUR POLITICAL INSTITUTIONS

Today our political institutions, and particularly Congress, are not working well at all, and the result is that we're far less able to deal with our differences than in the past.

One reason for this is that the dominance of the executive branch (the presidency), combined with the hollowing out of the legislative branch (Congress), leaves many people feeling as if they're shut out of the process.[3] Citizens of every political persuasion need to feel their views are being represented, particularly in a political environment in which there is so little trust. The political scientist Greg Weiner argues that presidential government exacerbates the problem of people feeling there's a lack of fair play in our politics because executive power is concentrated in a single person. He compares Congress to a 42-megapixel camera in that, because it consists of 535 people, Congress can register the full range of views among the people. The president, on the other hand, is more like a single pixel: you're either in or you're out. Republicans had no chance of their views being represented in the Obama administration, for example, and that's a problem from the perspective of fair play *if* the presidency dominates the system, as it now does. That's true of Democrats in the Trump administration. By contrast, anyone in the mainstream has a reasonable chance of their views being taken into account in Congress.

Right now our politics is dominated by the presidency, which is seen as the be-all and end-all of American politics.[4] A rebalancing between the executive and legislative branches is therefore needed. This is an argument for Congress to revitalize itself, to act as the first branch of government, and in the words of the government scholar Philip Wallach, "to understand its own proper purposes again." According to Wallach:

> If the political developments of the last few years have taught us nothing else, they have made one thing amply clear: America is a deeply divided nation, whose citizens sometimes seem to inhabit different moral universes. This makes it all the more important that we rely on a system of government that allows provisional cooperation between seemingly opposed factions. In our system, that means giving a prominent place to Congress.[5]

What that entails in practical terms includes structural reforms in Congress intended to compel more traditional legislative work and bargaining—for example, breaking up the budget process into smaller parts, in order to give Congress a chance to do more practical legislating in an ongoing way; combining authorizing and appropriating, which would enable members to exercise more authority over their domain and better tie the budget process to policy making; and allowing committees control of floor time, which would enable much more legislation to actually get to a vote.

It should involve giving Congress a greater role in oversight of executive and regulatory agencies and reforming campaign finance to reverse some of the errors of the past four decades, such as the strict limits on donations to parties that have empowered outside groups intent on activating the most polarized activists. We should also re-empower the parties as funders and take steps to liberate individual members to function as legislators representing their districts. When they work, the parties encourage the formation of broad coalitions, while individual members forced to become full-time fundraisers are more driven to please narrow interest groups. These kinds of reforms wouldn't exactly prevent confrontation or conflict in Washington. Rather, they would harness it to drive accommodation and give the people involved some incentives to build coalitions.

Professor Weiner makes the additional point that the media inevitably call any argument in Congress "bickering," and that form of thinking has infected public opinion. We tend to think of the job of Congress as legislating and passing bills, so when it doesn't, we assume the system has failed. "I would describe the job of Congress as representation and deliberation, such that deciding not to pass a bill is as 'productive' an action as deciding to pass one," he says. Some things will not and, indeed, should not pass—not because of venality or institutional failure but sometimes based on the merit and because of public opinion.

"There is no instance I can recall of a persistent majority in America not eventually getting what they want," according to Weiner. "Our constant resort to corruption as an explanation for any outcome we do not like exacerbates this problem. Increasingly, our opponents are not just wrong but corrupt and stupid because our own opinions are self-evidently right. The fragmentation of media just makes it worse."[6]

What we've lost sight of, it seems, is the understanding that conflicting points of view are not failure. Congress exists to legislate, of course, but also to facilitate debate and ultimately accommodation. It's an arena for *contained conflict*.

We can't eliminate political passions, then; what we need is to find a way to govern them. Well-functioning political institutions are essential to that task—but they are hardly sufficient. Democracy, after all, is about much more than procedures and structures. Underneath the procedures and structures there has to exist a certain civic ethic. To survive our system of government requires that the citizenry prize and embody certain democratic virtues, foremost among them *moderation*, *compromise*, and *civility*.

This troika has to once again become a part of our social fabric, the habits of the democratic heart. That begins with reacquainting ourselves with what these virtues are, and are not, and reminding ourselves of why they matter.

THE DEMOCRATIC VIRTUE OF MODERATION

At the outset of the Trump presidency, it was clear that it would be unpredictable in many ways, but there was one thing that could be reasonably counted on: moderation, an ancient virtue, would be viewed by many people with contempt. After all, the most temperamentally immoderate major party nominee in American history ran for president and won because of it. Victory spawns imitation, and the Trump template is likely to influence our politics for some time to come.

Moderation, then, is out of step with the times, which are characterized by populist anger and widespread anxiety, by cross-partisan animosity and dogmatic certainty. Those with whom we have political disagreements are not only wrong; they are often judged to be evil and irredeemable.

The difficulty is that in such a poisonous political culture, when moderation is the treatment we need to cleanse America's civic toxins, it invariably becomes synonymous with weakness, lack of conviction, and timidity. For many, moderation is what the French existentialist Jean-Paul Sartre called a "tender souls philosophy."

This is a serious problem, as Aurelian Craiutu argues in *Faces of Moderation: The Art of Balance in an Age of Extremes*, in which he profiles several prominent twentieth-century thinkers.[7] Mr. Craiutu, a professor of political science at Indiana University, argues that the success of representative government and its institutions depends on moderation. We therefore need political leaders to once again make the case for political moderation—but that requires untangling some misconceptions.

Moderation does not mean that truth is always found equidistant between two extreme positions, nor does it mean that bold steps aren't necessary to advance moral ends, nor that political actors eschew strong and principled convictions. Moderation takes into account what is needed at any given moment; it allows circumstances to determine action in the way that weather patterns dictate which route a ship will follow.

But there are general characteristics we associate with moderation, including prudence, the humility to recognize limits (those of others and our own), the willingness to balance competing principles, and an aversion to fanaticism. The most notable "philosophers of moderation," from Aristotle to Montaigne to Burke, stressed the role of moderation in taming the passions. What we need to strive for is proportionality, balance, the golden mean. *Meden Agan*, "nothing in excess," is the inscription of the temple of Apollo at Delphi. When that is ignored, catastrophe often follows.

It's worth noting that the American Revolution—unlike the French and Russian Revolutions—was characterized by moderation. In important respects it was a revolution to be sure, and as such was a radical break—most especially in arguing that liberty be made the end of government. But as Alexis de Tocqueville wrote, the revolution in America "was the result of a mature and reflecting preference for freedom, and not of a vague or ill-defined craving for independence. It contracted no alliance with the turbulent passions of anarchy, but its course was marked, on the contrary, by a love of order and law."[8]

The political theorist Martin Diamond, in his lecture "The Revolution of Sober Expectations," put it this way:

The makers of the American Revolution did not think themselves in possession of the simple and complete political truth, capable of instant application as a panacea for government. They claimed possession of only half the truth, namely, the self-evident truth that equal freedom must be the foundation of all political society. And in the name of that equal freedom they made half a revolution. But, soberly and moderately, they left open the question of institutions of government. These they knew would have to be forged from old materials, perhaps worked and reworked, and with a cool awareness that the new American institutions would be subject still to perennial human frailty and folly.[9]

The "half revolution" that began in 1776 reached its completion a decade later, in the framing and ratification of the Constitution, according to Diamond. The "noble sentiments" of Jefferson, author of the Declaration of Independence, combined with the "theoretic wisdom" of Madison, the chief designer of the Constitution. The American Revolution would succeed in ways in which others had failed.

Moderation accepts the complexity of life in this world and distrusts utopian visions and simple solutions. The way to think about moderation is as a disposition, not as an ideology. Its antithesis is not conviction but intemperance.

Moderates are wary of absolutism and turning politics into a Manichaean struggle pitting the forces of light against the forces of darkness. This approach allows us to remain open to facts that challenge our assumptions, and it makes us more likely to engage in debate free of invective.

"There are truths to be discovered, but truths complex and many-sided," in the words of Harry Clor, author of *On Moderation*. "The best way to get at them is by engaging contrary ideas in a manner approximating dialogue."[10]

Here I want to address head-on a charge that is often bandied about: moderates lack courage. That claim is easily put to rest by people like the twentieth-century French journalist and philosopher Raymond Aron. He was a man of deep, reasoned convictions who possessed a sense of proportion. A nonconformist, Aron was fearless in taking on the leading intellectuals of his time, including his friend Jean-Paul Sartre. (Parisian students in 1968 avowed that it was "better to be wrong with Sartre than right with Aron.") Aron strongly defended liberal democracy when denigrating it was fashionable.

For Aron, political moderation was a fighting creed. Allergic to ideological thinking, he worked to conform his views to evidence. He retained his intellectual and political independence throughout his life. Aron believed that history teaches us humility, modesty, and the limits of our knowledge. He was also skilled at the art of dialogue, engaging those he disagreed with critically but civilly. Aron put it this way: "Freedom flourishes in temperate zones; it does not survive the burning faith of prophets and crowds."[11]

Even before Mr. Trump set foot on the political stage, America was becoming a bit more like the Sahara or the Arctic Circle than a temperate zone. Moderation was passé in both parties, and no politician would defend it as a political virtue. So perhaps in retrospect it was almost inevitable that someone like Mr. Trump, who is "passion's slave," would rise up. Yet the business of a government, the philosopher Michael Oakeshott said, is "not to inflame passion and give it new objects to feed upon, but to inject into the activities of already too passionate men an ingredient of moderation."[12]

I'll readily concede that moderation is a difficult virtue for people to rally around, since by definition it doesn't arouse fervor or zealous advocates. But in a time of spreading resentment and rage—when truth is increasingly the target of assault, when dialogue is often viewed as duplicity, and when our ability to deal with our deep differences sometimes seems almost beyond our reach—moderation isn't simply a decorous democratic quality; it is an essential democratic virtue.

THE DEMOCRATIC VIRTUE OF COMPROMISE

If moderation is a disposition, then compromise—the settlement of differences through mutual concessions—is its practical manifestation. And like moderation, compromise is out of favor with a lot of people these days, at least with many of those who are most politically engaged and make up the base of the Republican and Democratic Parties. (Polling evidence suggests Republicans are more opposed to compromise as a concept than Democrats.)

The opposition to compromise can be explained by several factors, including hyperpolarization in our politics, which creates an atmosphere in which compromise is viewed as betrayal; the belief that our political opponents are determined to destroy America, meaning that compromise amounts to treason; and the emergence in politics of what is referred to as the "permanent campaign," meaning the next campaign begins as soon as the last campaign ends. This encourages what the scholars Amy Gutmann and Dennis Thompson refer to as "the uncompromising mindset," one that is conducive to campaigning but disastrous when it comes to governing, which requires give-and-take and deal making.[13]

In addition, opponents of compromise, like the Tea Party movement, which was a significant political force early in this decade, believe that compromise has harmed the country. The critics of compromise believe it is in almost every instance synonymous with lack of principles.

In some cases, of course, it is. Some people compromise on principle rather than being willing in principle to compromise. And it's impossible to judge the merits of compromise without knowing what was given and what was gained. The details make all the difference. It's also possible to become so enchanted with the idea of compromise that we undervalue or, in the name of compromise, erode the principles that ennoble politics. But as with moderation, there are a lot of wrong ideas about compromise that need to be unknotted.

For one thing, the premise that one's political opponents are out to destroy America is not only ungracious but paranoid. It's true that some people are driven by ill will and a malicious contempt for the United States, but that's hardly representative. The starting point should be that those with whom we disagree differ over the means to the end, but the end we seek is essentially the same: a better and more just society.

That doesn't mean that conservatives and liberals don't place different weight on different values—for example, respect for authority as against those whose impulse is to challenge authority, or emphasizing equality of opportunity over equality of outcome. But the burden of proof has to be on those who claim that those who hold a different ideology than they do are intent on hurting America, and it's generally not one they can meet.

As for the claim that compromise is for the fainthearted, John F. Kennedy, in his book *Profiles in Courage*, answered it this way: "Compromise does not mean cowardice. Indeed it is frequently the compromisers and conciliators who are faced with the severest tests of political courage as they oppose the extremist views of their constituents." Kennedy went on to point out that lawmakers who have contempt heaped on them for compromising are often doing what they are meant to do: "Engaged in the fine art of conciliating, balancing and interpreting the forces and factions of public opinion, an art essential to keeping our nation united and enabling our Government to function."[14]

Undergirding the case for compromise is the recognition that none of us is perfect and very few political issues are uncomplicated, with only good arguments and the angels lined up on one side and only bad arguments and demons lined up on the other.

Compromise is the result of "our insurmountable lack of perfect knowledge," one political theorist told me. None of us has all the answers.

The nineteenth-century leader of the Whig Party, Henry Clay—who served in the House of Representatives, in the Senate, and was a secretary of state under John Adams—was one of the most influential members of Congress in American history. Known as "the Great Compromiser," he played a vital role in formulating compromises on some of the great sectional issues of his time: the Missouri Compromise (1820), the Tariff Compromise (1833), and the Compromise of 1850. He offered up this defense of compromise:

All legislation, all government, all society is founded upon the principle of mutual concession, politeness, comity, courtesy; upon these everything is based. . . . Let him who elevates himself above humanity, above its weaknesses, its infirmities, its wants, its necessities, say, if he pleases, I will never compromise; but let no one who is not above the frailties of our common nature disdain compromises.[15]

Since none of us is above the frailties of our common nature, reflexive disdain for compromise is both unwarranted and unwise.

But there is a still more positive case that can be made on behalf of compromise.

In an essay for *National Affairs* magazine, Jonathan Rauch of the Brookings Institution writes in praise of compromise, saying that "in our constitutional system, compromise is not merely a necessary evil but a positive good: an indispensable source of political discipline, competition and stability." In encourages incremental progress, accommodation, and reform that has bipartisan investment. It also rejects the seductive appeal of the absolute.

Rauch argues that compromise is part of the Madisonian framework—"the most essential principle of our constitutional system." He adds, "Those who hammer out painful deals perform the hardest and, often, highest work of politics; they deserve, in general, respect for their willingness to constructively advance their ideals, not condemnation for treachery."[16]

This observation can be best illustrated by studying the Constitutional Convention, which led to the ratification of the Constitution. How this series of events came to pass is among the more extraordinary stories in human history.

"It appears to me, then, little short of a miracle," Washington wrote to Lafayette on February 7, 1788, "that the Delegates from so many different States (which States you know are also different from each other in their manners, circumstances and prejudices) should unite in forming a system of national Government, so little liable to well founded objections."[17]

Compromise was key to this miracle. For example, the Constitutional Convention was deadlocked and on the verge of being derailed until the so-called Grand Compromise—offered up by Roger Sherman and Oliver Ellsworth—reconciled the interests of small and large states. (Each state's House members would be elected by the people and based on state population, while each state would be represented by two senators chosen by the state legislatures.)

"After the Great Compromise many more issues had to be resolved, but by now a spirit of accommodation had developed," according to the scholars John J. DiIulio Jr. and the late James Q. Wilson.[18] The electoral college was the result of compromise; so was determining how Supreme Court justices were picked and the length of time a president could serve. And then there was the thorniest issue of all, slavery.

The southern delegates would never have supported the new Constitution if it meant the abolition of slavery. And so compromises were made in terms of representation (the South wanted slaves counted as full persons to increase white southern representation in Congress; eventually slaves were considered three-fifths of a person); in terms of delaying the prohibition on the importation of slaves (until the year 1808); and in dealing with escaped slaves (those who fled to nonslave states would be returned to their masters if caught).

Slavery was a moral obscenity—but the delegates concluded

that, in the words of Madison, "great as the evil is, a dismemberment of the union would be worse." What the more enlightened founders hoped was that the Constitution would put in place the elements to end slavery. Frederick Douglass, the former slave who became a great abolitionist leader, would later say, "Interpreted as it ought to be interpreted, the Constitution is a GLORIOUS LIBERTY DOCUMENT."[19]

In her splendid book *Miracle at Philadelphia*, Catherine Drinker Bowen captures the drama and suspense, the intense arguments and the despair, and the moments of high purpose and nobility. She also captures the voices of the delegates—including some of the most notable names in American history (Washington, Madison, Hamilton, and Franklin, as well as some lesser-known ones like John Dickinson, James Wilson, and Gouverneur Morris)—who gathered in secret sessions from May through September 1787, not to revise the Articles of Confederation, which was the stated purpose, but to write a new constitution.

"The situation of this Assembly, groping as it were in the dark to find political truth," is how eighty-one-year-old Benjamin Franklin described it. And what a political truth they found. The governing charter they created has become the longest-enduring written national constitution in the world and among the greatest political achievements ever.

But it was not just human intellect that carried the day in Philadelphia; it was the product of a certain kind of human character. Ms. Bowen describes it this way:

> The Federal Convention, viewed from the records, is startlingly fresh and "new." The spirit behind it was the spirit of compromise, seemingly no very noble flag to rally round.

Compromise can be an ugly word, signifying a pact with the devil, a chipping off of the best to suit the worst. Yet in the Constitutional Convention the spirit of compromise reigned in grace and glory; as Washington presided, it sat on his shoulder like the dove. Men rise to speak and one sees them struggle with the bias of birthright, locality, statehood—South against North, East against West, merchant against planter. One sees them change their minds, fight against pride, and when the moment comes, admit their error.[20]

The founders were imperfect men, and the Constitution an imperfect document. But all things considered, what happened at Independence Hall was little short of a miracle. And for a group of fiercely proud and independent individuals to rise above such deep difference for the sake of the public good, to compromise in order to advance justice and human dignity, was a rare and wonderful thing. It's something worth aspiring to in our time, when excellence and high-mindedness in public life seem to be hidden away on distant hills.

THE DEMOCRATIC VIRTUE OF CIVILITY

We live in an era of growing incivility. We can see it and sense it all around us, from the rudeness we encounter while driving and shopping to social media posts and cyberbullying to cable television and talk radio to the behavior of the politicians and, preeminently, the president of the United States.

A 2017 survey found "a severe civility deficit in our nation"[21]— and there are no signs of it letting up. Among the findings: the belief that the US has a major civility problem has reached a record high (69 percent); three-quarters of Americans believe that incivility has risen to crisis levels; and the same proportion feels that the US is losing stature as a civil nation (73 percent).

Nearly nine in ten Americans say incivility leads to intimidation and threats, violence, cyberbullying, and harassment. Nearly 80 percent say that uncivil comments by political leaders encourage greater incivility in society, while nearly 60 percent say they quit paying attention to politics because of incivility.

"The feeling that politicians are at the root of our society's spreading incivility runs deep," according to the survey.

"Americans are worried about the consequences of the incivility that has infected all aspects of our society," according to Jack Leslie, chairman of Weber Shandwick, one of the firms that conducted the research.

They're right to worry. Incivility not only implies disrespect, discourteousness, and impoliteness; it derives from the Latin word *incivilis*, meaning "not of a citizen." To be uncivil, then, is to act in ways that tend to put one at odds with what it means to be a responsible citizen.

The converse is also true: *civility is central to citizenship*. It is the precondition, not the product, of respect for others. When civility is stripped away, everything in life becomes a battlefield, an arena for conflict, an excuse for invective. Families, communities, our conversations, and our institutions break apart when basic civility is absent. Everyday life becomes nearly intolerable.

But like moderation and compromise, civility is a widely misunderstood virtue. In the eyes of many people, it's synonymous with lack of conviction and passion. To be a civilized individual, according to this line of reasoning, means to be delicate and pliable, devoid of principles, unwilling to fight for great causes.

This is confusion of a high order. It takes but a moment's consideration to realize that one can be a vigorous and forceful advocate for justice without being uncivil. Nor does civility mean we don't speak the truth. It doesn't mean we fail to call things by their rightful name or refuse to call out nonsense when we see it. A person can be both civil and angry at injustice; Martin Luther King Jr. showed that as well as anyone in recent American history. Yale professor Stephen L. Carter, in his book on civility, said that "the true genius of Martin Luther King, Jr. was not his ability to articulate the pain of an oppressed people—many other preachers did so, with as much passion and as much power—but in his ability to inspire those very people to be loving and civil in their dissent."[22]

What civility makes possible is a certain mode of discourse, particularly when it comes to debates and disagreements with our fellow citizens. It assumes that in most cases—absent fairly extraordinary exceptions—basic good manners are what we owe others as fellow citizens and fellow human beings, even those with whom we have passionate disagreements. Undergirding this belief for many of us is the conviction that we're all image-bearers of God—"a work of divine art" in the words of the theologian Richard Mouw—which demands that we respect human dignity.

"Let your conversation be always full of grace, seasoned with salt," Saint Paul wrote in his letter to the Colossians, "so that you may know how to answer everyone." And to the Galatians, Paul describes the "fruits of the spirit" as love, joy, peace, forbearance, kindness, goodness, faithfulness, gentleness, and self-control.

Incivility is notably left off the list.

Civility helps inoculate us against the temptation to dehumanize those who hold views different from our own. Civility is, as Carter has written, a precondition of democratic dialogue. Finding common ground and reaching accommodation is hard enough when opposing worldviews collide; it's impossible to achieve when the rhetoric each side uses against the other is laced with venom and contempt. The survival of a functioning parliamentary system, Sir William Harcourt said, depends on "constant dining with the opposition."[23]

We often (and unfairly) assume our differences are the result of the other person's moral failures or of them acting in bad faith. In reality, it's more often a case of us placing different emphasis on values like authority and diversity, stability and change. That doesn't mean we'll agree on everything, but it does mean we might understand others a little better, see a little more clearly how they arrived at their position, and be a little less harsh in our assessment of those with whom we have deep differences.

As a lifelong conservative, I'm dismayed to see how certain figures in the American Right have turned conservatism into a cavalcade of insults and now denigrate civility. A few years ago Craig Shirley, a public affairs consultant and author of bestselling biographies of Ronald Reagan and an authorized biography of Newt Gingrich, wrote an essay, "In Defense of Incivility." In it he insisted that civility is not only overrated but an outright threat to American democracy, "the last thing we need in American politics."[24] He argues that civility is a "way to control the citizenry, by shaming them into silence when focused anger would serve the Republic better." Civility, he says, is unconservative and un-American, while American conservatism is "uncivil and intellectual." Indeed, he adds, civility permits many great evils, while incivility is the source of many wonders for which we should be grateful. "Three cheers for American incivility," is how Shirley put it. (It was no surprise that he praised Donald Trump's incivility and anger as contributions to the 2016 presidential contest.) The popular radio talk show host Mark Levin eagerly echoed Shirley's criticisms of civility.[25]

One need only contrast Shirley and Levin with two of the most important figures in conservatism in the latter half of the twentieth century, Ronald Reagan and William F. Buckley Jr., who were renowned for their grace, class, and good manners. They were remarkably and blessedly free of roiling resentments.

While often the target of vicious attacks, Reagan maintained a remarkably charitable view of his political adversaries. "Remember, we have no enemies, only opponents," former Indiana governor Mitch Daniels, who worked as a political aide in the Reagan White House, quotes him as admonishing his staff. Even Mr. Reagan's rare flashes of anger did not cross lines of decency or turn ad hominem.

As for Mr. Buckley: in a heated 1968 televised exchange with the left-wing writer Gore Vidal, Buckley defended the police in the aftermath of violent encounters with protesters during the Democratic Convention. Vidal called Buckley a "crypto-Nazi." This enraged Buckley, who had served in World War II, and he referred to Vidal as a "queer." Buckley said that if Vidal didn't cease referring to him as a "crypto-Nazi," "I'll sock you in your goddamn face, and you'll stay plastered."[26]

This was a jarring, incongruous moment for a man renowned for his elegance and gentlemanliness. Andrew Ferguson, writing in the *Weekly Standard*, said that for the rest of his life, Buckley "admitted to being ashamed of the moment—not merely for the lapse in manners but for allowing so crude a provocation to produce exactly the effect Vidal intended."[27]

But the great model to look to here, as he is in so many areas, is Lincoln. As a young man, it is said, his satirical inclination and self-confident polemical power provided him with the "power to hurt." But as he matured, his biographer William Lee Miller has written, "one can almost observe him curbing that inclination and becoming scrupulous and respectful."[28] His personal and professional dealings—with clients, editors, supporters, and opponents—had a "distinct quality of tact, generosity, and civility."[29]

But note well: the way to reclaim civility is *not* by having liberals lecture conservatives about their lack of civility and comity, and vice versa. This typically inflames passions rather than calming things down ("Who the hell are *they* to lecture *me*? Remove the mote in your own eye before complaining about the speck in mine"). Instead it has to start with self-reflection and looking within—first at ourselves as individuals, then at the parties and political movements we are part of.

All of us, but particularly our political leaders, need to challenge those with whom we share a common ideology to examine our own blind spots, to cease assuming that those who hold different views than we do have nothing to teach us, and to stop demonizing and degrading our political opponents. To put it another way: we need people *within* our own political tribe to point out the dangers of excessive political tribalism, one of which includes incivility.

The twentieth-century Scottish writer John Buchan, who had a career in politics, put it beautifully when he wrote:

While I believed in party government and in party loyalty, I never attained to the happy partisan zeal of many of my friends, being painfully aware of my own and my party's defects, and uneasily conscious of the merits of my opponent. Like Montaigne I could forgive "neither the commendable qualities of my adversaries nor the reproachful of those I followed."[30]

Now think about the times you've gotten into heated political debates with other people, including your friends. It might be on abortion or gay rights, immigration or gun violence. What's often going on is that we're frustrated to the point of anger because the other person won't jettison their views and adopt ours. The feeling is, "I'm right, he's wrong, and he's being unreasonable in not conceding I'm right." The point of debate, after all, is to convince others of the merits of my arguments and the weakness of theirs. If my argument isn't working, my natural reflex is to repeat the same argument, this time increasing the volume, the vehemence, and the agitation.

It never works—in fact, it almost always backfires. We have to find a better way.

In May 2017, I had a series of email exchanges with a nationally recognized conservative commentator, someone I had known for several years and always gotten along well with. But there were inevitable tensions, given that I was a vocal Trump critic and he was a vocal Trump defender.

In this particular instance, he was unhappy with a column I had written that was critical of Donald Trump, and in the course of our exchange he leveled several charges against me. My initial impulse was to answer them with a blunt, point-by-point refutation.

I thought, "I was *born* to respond to accusations like this." But as I reflected on it, I decided doing so would be a mistake. No matter how strong the arguments I marshaled on behalf of my case—and they would probably not be as strong as I thought they were—they simply wouldn't be heard by him. It was also bound to hurt the relationship, making him feel under assault and therefore defensive. So I tried a different approach.

I admitted to my interlocutor that my strong aversion to Donald Trump made me susceptible to being unfair in my judgment of him. And rather than answer his charges, I went on to explain, in as detached and fair-minded a manner as I could, our competing perspectives. After having done so, I said this:

> What I think is happening with the two of us is we're placing emphasis on different values/perceived virtues. You're asking for loyalty, which keeps you from criticizing Trump (because, in part, you don't want to be on the side of people on the Left/Trump haters for whom you have disdain); I'm asking for intellectual honesty, which means using the same standard on Trump you'd use on HRC [Hillary Rodham Clinton] or Obama, and giving voice to criticisms when you honestly believe the criticisms are warranted. This explains why you get frustrated with me for (in your eyes) being disloyal and being a willing participant in the anti-Trump mob; while I get frustrated with you for (in my eyes) not showing intellectual honesty when it comes to Trump, for not saying things that you privately know to be true.

What's notable is his response, which was not angry but self-reflective. He expressed genuine gratitude for our friendship and said, "I received everything you said tonight fully. In fact, I read over your note a couple of times. And I've had one of those cathartic moments. I believe the disconnect you and I experience regarding Trump world is the difference between objectivity and subjectivity."

"You endeavor to be objective," he told me, adding, "it hit me like a ton of bricks: I have no desire to be objective. That's my blind spot, I suppose. I'm not a journalist, I'm an opinion guy." He felt like Donald Trump was being lacerated by the elite media on a daily basis, and he saw his job as defending Trump in every instance and giving Trump supporters a safe harbor in the form of his show.

"I don't think that makes either of us right or wrong," he wrote me. "I'm self-aware enough to know that just because I disagree with you doesn't make me right or you wrong. We're just approaching this wild ride quite differently from one another."

He was right, and a decade or so earlier, I would likely have taken this exchange in a different and more negative direction. In this case, though, the tone was reasonably civil and respectful, and as a result, we have continued to stay engaged with each other. We're able to understand each other's perspective somewhat better, even if neither of us has been converted to the other side of the divide.

The following year, I heard his program while driving on the George Washington Memorial Parkway in Virginia, heading in to my office in Washington, DC. I noticed that he instructed his listeners—almost all of whom are pro-Trump and pro–Second Amendment—not to be personally harsh toward the students of Marjory Stoneman Douglas High School in Parkland, Florida, who were leading a gun control campaign in the aftermath of a massacre at their school. I sent him a note commending him.

"I was impressed with what you said," I wrote, "about having sympathy and understanding for the students who were critical of the NRA without agreeing with them." I added, "My guess is that there were more than a few people in your audience who felt like you were going 'soft' and sounding like a 'RINO' [Republican in name only]."

He wrote a gracious note back to me, which included this statement: "By the way, you should know that your voice has an impact on me."

DEVELOPING SECOND FRIENDS

What too many of us have lost sight of—what from time to time *I've* lost sight of—is that the purpose of political discourse and debate shouldn't be to score partisan points, to get in good shots and a clever put-down now and then, or even to be proven right. In fact, the purpose of debate is to better ascertain truth and reality—and that's often done by refining and amending our views as a result of scrutiny, dialogue, and debate. It's just a very different way of approaching things.

One excellent illustration of this is the friendship between Owen Barfield, a British philosopher and poet, and C. S. Lewis, the twentieth-century British medievalist, literary critic, and essayist, and author of the children's series The Chronicles of Narnia.

Lewis and Barfield met at Oxford; they were close friends for more than forty years and members of the literary group the Inklings. Both men of the Christian faith, they exercised enormous influence on each other—Lewis dedicated his first scholarly book, *The Allegory of Love*, to Barfield, the "wisest and best of my unofficial teachers"—but their friendship was not based on seeing the world in exactly the same way. In fact, they engaged in some fairly intense disagreements, including on the relationship between imagination and truth (an epistolary exchange affectionately dubbed "the Great War").

Lewis described what he called a "First Friend" and a "Second Friend." The First Friend is your alter ego, the person who sees things as you do. You "join like raindrops on a window," in Lewis's words.

The Second Friend is not your alter ego but rather your anti-self. He shares your interests but approaches them at a different angle. "He has read all the right books but has got the wrong thing out of every one," Lewis wrote. "How can he be so nearly right and yet, invariably, just not right?"

> You go at it, hammer and tongs, far into the night, or walking through fine country that neither gives a glance to, each learning the weight of the other's punches, and often more like mutually respectful enemies than friends. Actually (though it never seems so at the time) you modify one another's thought; out of this perpetual dogfight a community of mind and a deep affection emerge.[31]

"In an argument," Barfield said, "we always, both of us, were arguing for the truth, not for victory."[32]

If we could move closer toward the spirit of the Lewis-Barfield model of dialogue and debate, we'd all be far better off. It would certainly help us think of our national politics as something other than a fight to the death.

These changes won't happen easily or quickly, but it's not beyond our capacity to achieve them. It's a matter of being purposeful, of thinking about the good of the whole. And if you think about it, that's really not too much to ask.

OUR DISTORTED VISION OF REALITY

The theologian Andrew Davison tells about being in India and coming across a person with leprosy. As a Christian, he saw the leper and felt compassion and aided him, though much to the unease of Indians. It then struck him that those who believe in karma and reincarnation, as Hindus do, see a leper as someone atoning for past sins and doing what needs to be done for a future, and better, reincarnation. So they interpreted aiding the leper as doing something inappropriate.

Davison wrote, "We do not first see neutrally, and then interpret. The leper is *seen as* unfortunate, as someone upon whom to show pity, or *seen as* a miscreant, as someone to be reviled. Axioms operate at this very direct level as well as in more discursive reasoning."[33]

This illustration is meant to show how our worldviews shape our interpretation of events and reality, to demonstrate how people can see the same situation and react to it in wholly different ways.

This doesn't mean that there is no such thing as objective truth. As I made abundantly clear in the previous chapter, I'm not a postmodernist. I don't believe reality is something that is simply shaped by interpretation, or that just because people sincerely hold a belief—like, say, reincarnation—it makes that belief true. But Davison's illustration does underscore a key attribute of responsible citizenship: forbearance for others and modesty toward ourselves.

Here's what I mean: most of us assume that people see issues—

abortion, same-sex marriage and transgenderism, gun control, tax policy and income inequality, entitlement reform, illegal immigration, welfare payments, climate change, Black Lives Matter, and countless others—through essentially the same prism we do. But it's more complicated than that.

Our interpretative frame and intellectual and moral tendencies are the product of many factors. The philosopher Cornelius Van Til once said that there is no such thing as a brute fact. Our presumptions alter the way we interpret things, including justice. For example, if one views abortion entirely through the lens of a woman's right to choose, then restricting abortions is a gratuitous offense. If one views abortion through the prism of the rights and well-being of an unborn child, on the other hand, then subsidizing abortion is a grave transgression.

Or take same-sex marriage. Some believe championing gay marriage places one on the side of equality, tolerance, and human dignity, as heirs of the civil rights struggle. On the flip side, opponents of gay marriage often root their views in their understanding of male-female complementarity, procreation, and the health of the institution of marriage. They are acting to defend what they believe are true and necessary social norms. The differences on this issue can be explained by reasons other than bigotry on the one hand or wanting to rip apart our social fabric on the other.

Too often, we tend to deny to those with whom we disagree any benefit of the doubt. We assume they see facts, events, and justice just as we do, which makes their differing conclusions very nearly inexplicable. This in turn makes it easy to characterize one's opponents as malignant, to think that only a cretin could hold views at odds with ours.

It would help improve our political culture if we understood that every one of us has an imperfect angle on reality and that truth is refracted by our presuppositions. Our perception of justice is always distorted, even if just a little bit. All of us see through a glass darkly and know things only in part.

George Orwell expressed this point in an exquisite way. His 1938 book *Homage to Catalonia* is a gripping account of his role in the Spanish Civil War, first as a journalist and then as a participant. Near the end of the book are these words:

> I hope the account I have given is not too misleading. I believe on such an issue as this no one is or can be completely truthful. It is difficult to be certain about anything except what you have seen with your own eyes, and consciously or unconsciously everyone writes as a partisan. In case I have not said this somewhere earlier in the book I will say it now: beware of my partisanship, my mistakes of fact and the distortion inevitably caused by my having seen only one corner of events. And beware of exactly the same thing when you read any other book on this period of the Spanish war.[34]

One cannot help but be struck by the honesty and self-knowledge, the acknowledgment that we all express ourselves as partisans to one degree or another and that distortions arise because we see "only one corner of events."

This doesn't mean that some people aren't much closer than others to apprehending truth, beauty, and goodness. Nor do I believe for a moment that efforts at persuasion are fruitless. I do believe, though, that greater tolerance toward the perspective of our political opponents is necessary for good citizenship; that in our hearts and minds forbearance and patience need to find a place alongside passionate convictions and persistence. If they do, our politics will be characterized by a touch more grace, a bit less anger, and a little more sympathy.

There are worse things in the world.

HOW CITIZENS CAN HEAL THE BREACH

To summarize, then: in a nation like the United States, composed of some 325 million people, there is no hope for widespread agreement, for common perspectives and easy common ground, on a vast range of issues. Democracy is not a machine that manufactures consent. The task of every generation is how to succeed given the reality of deep differences. So what practically does that mean? What can actually be done?

For one thing, Americans can support people running for public office who model what respectful, civil disagreements look like. We can also oppose those who are the antithesis of moderation, compromise, and civility. Registering opposition to those who summon forth our darkest instincts is especially important when it is directed at people you otherwise agree with. It's easy to vote against someone whose policies and political philosophy you already disagree with; the most effective dissent is when it's aimed at those you generally align with.

Those in public life will conform their behavior to what their constituents demand and reward. If enough people are fed up with the politics of intemperance and incivility, they need to make it a priority to vote for men and women who offer an alternative. It may seem banal, but core truths often are; and the quickest route to changing our political culture is by voting into office people who conduct themselves with decency and class.

But to merely say we need to vote better people into office is simplistic and insufficient. Our politics is venomous because some large number of Americans want it to be that way. What we're seeing is one manifestation of civic rot. How to reverse that is a more complicated, longer-term task.

For starters, we need to shut down the sophisticated disinformation operations run by foreign governments, in particular Russia. Their purpose is to sow discord as a means of undermining the United States. Platforms like Facebook and Twitter were built in a way that easily allowed for mass manipulation. Russian operatives from the Kremlin-linked group Internet Research Agency (IRA) flooded them with bots and fake accounts to spread divisive narratives, especially during elections and in order to elect Donald Trump. According to a December 2018 report prepared for the Senate Intelligence Committee, Russia's IRA activities were designed to polarize the US public and interfere in elections by

- campaigning for African American voters to boycott elections or follow the wrong voting procedures in 2016, and more recently for Mexican American and Hispanic voters to distrust US institutions;
- encouraging extreme right-wing voters to be more confrontational; and
- spreading sensationalist, conspiratorial, and other forms of junk political news and misinformation to voters across the political spectrum.[35]

The journalist Sara Fischer summarized things this way: the news about "Russia's online disinformation efforts suggest that all of the major social media platforms, ranging from Facebook and Google's empires to Reddit and Tumblr, were weaponized over the past two years."[36]

Social media platforms are hurting democracy; they need to be held accountable, and they need to be fixed. There should be a much greater public outcry about this, and Americans of both parties should pressure Congress to do more to regulate these industries. There is enough acrimony in American politics today without having foreign adversaries stirring up more.

At a more fundamental level, education is surely part of the answer. This starts with more emphasis on civic literacy as a way to improve civic knowledge and shape democratic attitudes. As the education scholar Robert Pondiscio reminds us, "The founding purpose of public education in America was not to advance the private end of college and career preparation, but the public purpose of ensuring that the nation's children would be able to participate fully and knowledgeably in civic life as adults."[37]

Part of civics education is knowing American history, which helps us to better understand our times, offers us clues on how to confront the problems we face, and reminds us that difficult times aren't unprecedented or impossible to overcome. It counteracts despair. History also provides us with flesh-and-blood examples of people who, in the face of great challenges, embodied qualities like moderation and compromise. And that's not all: a greater knowledge of history will revive our identity as Americans, connecting us to the past, to our founding principles and our failures, and to one another.

Unfortunately civics education today is in sorry shape and has been for some time; it has become "little more than a rote study of the structures of government."[38] Ignorance of history and the basics of government is rather astounding. For example, one quarter of Americans can name the three branches of government (executive, legislative, and judiciary); if you're unfamiliar with that, it makes it impossible to understand the importance of checks and balances and the separation of powers.[39] When asked in what century the American Revolution took place, more than a third did not know; and half of respondents believed that either the Civil War, the War of 1812, or the Emancipation Proclamation occurred before the American Revolution.[40] Less than a third of American students in grades four, eight, and twelve are "proficient" in civics, meaning in "the knowledge, skills, attitudes, and experiences to prepare someone to be an active, informed participant in democratic life."[41]

In his 1986 Jefferson Lecture, the Polish philosopher and historian of ideas Leszek Kolakowski spoke about what he termed the "erosion of historical consciousness" and our "historical self-understanding sinking into irrelevance or oblivion." Kolakowski said that we learn history not just to know who we are but to learn what we are responsible for and how this responsibility should play itself out. History connects us with the past, with tradition, with community. The loss of knowledge of history, he warned, "plays havoc" with the lives of the young and "threatens their ability to withstand possible trials in the future."[42] A sense of history, then, prepares us for democratic citizenship—and not knowing history means we are failing in our duties as citizens.

Fortunately there are groups like the Civics Renewal Network, a consortium of nonpartisan, nonprofit organizations committed to strengthening civic life in the US.[43] One of those organizations is iCivics, founded in 2009 by former Supreme Court justice Sandra Day O'Connor. It teaches students about government through online, interactive games and supporting classroom resources, and the result is more active and informed citizens. The overwhelming number of teachers who use it report that it fosters civil conversations about current events in their classrooms. (iCivics is now the largest provider of civics curricula in the nation, reaching nearly 200,000 teachers and more than 5 million students, in all fifty states.)

The leverage here is parents, who can encourage and insist that state and local policy makers put a renewed focus on citizenship education. It's not as if the material doesn't exist; it's a matter of insisting that the material be taught.

There's more that can be done. We can revitalize summer leadership and citizenship programs like Boys State and Girls State, which are sponsored by the American Legion and the American Legion Auxiliary. They are basically weeklong simulations of state and local government for high school students. They show teenagers how challenging and exciting it can be to try to work together to formulate and generate support for "policies" that address a common problem. Those who participate are expected to debate ideas while staying civil; all participants are immersed in the ideals of a democracy while also getting a taste of the frustrations. In their heyday, Boys State and Girls State were some of the best programs in helping young people understand the worth, effort, and challenges of citizenship.

Another area that offers some hope is voluntary national service. National service, in addition to helping repair broken communities and broken lives through the service itself, also instills a sense of purpose and patriotism and connects people of different classes, ethnicities, races, and life experiences. When people work together side by side for a common purpose, political differences are deintensified. According to a study by the Panetta Institute for Public Policy, "Participants of all races and backgrounds describe how their service has taught them new perspectives and approaches, and exposed them to groups of people with whom they would not have identified in the past."[44]

In his 1990 book *Gratitude: Reflections on What We Owe to Our Country*, one of the founders of modern conservatism, William F. Buckley Jr., who was introduced earlier, called for a year of voluntary national service for young people eighteen and over, in areas such as health, day care, and the environment, to strengthen their feeling and appreciation for their nation. "Materialistic democracy beckons every man to make himself a king; republican citizenship incites every man to be a knight," Buckley wrote.[45] Service to one's country calls forth "the better angels within our nature" and can "ever so slightly elevate us from the trough of self-concern and self-devotion." Harkening back to his experience in World War II, Buckley refers to the close affinity that united the "Laramie cowboy" and the "college-campus litterateur in Greenwich Village."[46]

SUPPORT CIVILITY PROJECTS

In a different realm, one of the encouraging developments in recent years is the creation of programs whose explicit mission is to model how people who disagree can do so responsibly and without rancor.

One such organization is Better Angels, a national citizens' movement to reduce political polarization by bringing liberals and conservatives together, face-to-face, to understand each other beyond stereotypes, forming red/blue community alliances and teaching practical skills for communicating across political differences. (More than a thousand people have participated in the workshops in more than thirty states.)[47] They build "zones of depolarization" in the form of workshops that allow people of different political viewpoints to listen to each other's opinions, values, and experiences. The result is that hard edges are sanded off and opportunities to compromise open up.

The founder of Better Angels, David Blankenhorn, says that the group's goal is "achieving disagreement." The goal is not to get people to change their views; it is to get people to *listen well* to one another. "If you listen," according to Blankenhorn, "and if you try to understand—and if you're confident that people are going to then listen to you—you become a human being, friendship develops despite the political differences, and the rancor goes down."

It sounds simplistic, Blankenhorn acknowledges, but "it's like magic." Their commitment is to bring people together "to talk across these differences as fellow citizens."[48]

"What we are trying to change," Blankenhorn says, "is how they think about each other as citizens." The goal is for people to return to their communities and put what they learned into practice. If enough people abide by these principles, the people associated with Better Angels believe, they can transform the country from the bottom up.

A similar program, Speak Your Peace: The Civility Project, was launched in Duluth, Minnesota, in 2003. The program was developed by the Duluth Superior Area Community Foundation in response to increasing political tensions caused by economic decline, plants closing, and rising anxiety. Agreement seemed out of reach on an array of issues; the mood was hot and contentious. "Rather than working on solutions we started fighting with each other," says Rob Karwath, former executive editor of the *Duluth News Tribune*.[49]

Holly Sampson, president of the foundation, said she was hearing from younger people in particular that they were hesitant to get involved in the public debate because it was so contentious. (A headline in the *Duluth News Tribune* read, "Divisiveness Stalls Projects and Keeps Some from Running for Office.")

The Speak Your Peace initiative connected older and younger generations in Duluth, and it was eagerly embraced across sectors, from government forums to middle school classrooms. Ms. Sampson said the foundation was "totally overwhelmed" by the community's response to the public campaign.[50]

"This is not a campaign to end disagreements," according to the website. "It is a campaign to improve public discourse by simply reminding ourselves of the very basic principles of respect."[51]

The nine rules for practicing civility that were adopted were taken from P. M. Forni's book *Choosing Civility*.

- **Pay attention.** Be aware and attend to the world and the people around you.
- **Listen.** Focus on others to better understand their points of view.
- **Be inclusive.** Welcome all groups of citizens working for the greater good of the community.
- **Don't gossip.** And don't accept when others choose to do so.
- **Show respect.** Honor other people and their opinions, especially in the midst of disagreement.

- **Be agreeable.** Look for opportunities to agree; don't contradict just to do so.
- **Apologize.** Be sincere and repair damaged relationships.
- **Give constructive criticism.** When disagreeing, stick to the issues and don't make a personal attack.
- **Take responsibility.** Don't shift responsibility and blame onto others; share disagreements publicly.

These nine rules for civility had such resonance that the Duluth public schools developed a curriculum that implemented them. Years after the initiative was started, people testified that there was a markedly positive change in the political climate, and the community followed that lead.

The *Wall Street Journal*'s Gerald Seib reports that Duluth's mayor, Emily Larson, credits the civility project for helping the city work through an emotional two-year debate over a new ordinance requiring employers to offer paid sick leave, which was adopted in May 2018.

Mayor Larson told Seib, "To me, civility is about truly listening." By actually listening, she says, people discover they have some common ground, which "lays the groundwork for the next conversation." According to Seib, "Duluth's experience is worth a look, if only because it shows that such a slide [toward mob violence] is neither inevitable nor unstoppable."[52] This kind of effort can be replicated in pretty much every community in America.

Both Better Angels and Speak Your Peace are examples of what public intellectuals like David Brooks and Yuval Levin refer to as constructive localism, which they believe offers the best way out of our current predicament.

The basic argument they make is that our national politics is deformed, the federal government is paralyzed and distrusted, and state and local governments are where much of the action is, where greater mutual trust resides, and where most of the solutions are to be found.

At the local level it's far easier to experiment and try innovative approaches (like charter schools) that are tailored to the needs of local communities. It's also in local communities that you deal with others person-to-person. As a result, politics is less distant, less impersonal, and therefore more humanizing. Nor is it filtered through hyperpartisan media outlets that have a ratings interest in keeping Americans in a constant state of agitation and rage. Local politics and civic engagement draw people out of their partisan silos. And if you believe, as I do, that one of the major problems facing America today is isolation and alienation, the loss of human connection and loving attachments, then the answer by definition has to be local. There's a human touch found at the local level that is impossible to replicate at the national level.

"A more interpersonal and local politics is . . . likely to be more civil more of the time," according to Levin, "lowering the temperature of our public life and enabling more accommodation than could be possible on the vast and impersonal scale of national political debates."[53]

This isn't to argue that national politics isn't important or that there are not some problems that only the national government can combat. But it *is* to argue that repairing our broken national politics begins with each of us being more involved in local politics and community service, an option that is available to almost all of us. It's a bottom-up approach that over time can change the political landscape of a nation.

You may feel largely powerless to change politics in Washington, DC, but you're not powerless to change politics where you live—in McLean, Virginia, or Pueblo, Colorado; in Richland, Washington, or Glendale, Arizona; in Bridgeport, Connecticut, or Huntsville, Alabama; or in any of the three thousand counties and twenty thousand cities across America.

You're certainly not powerless to connect with and serve the people in your neighborhood—to become exposed to their worlds, to find out more about their lives, to listen to their perspectives, to learn from their experiences, and to lend a helping and healing hand.

And you're certainly not powerless to model civility, temperance, humility, tolerance, honesty, compassion, decency, and grace in your home life and at work, in your relationships with your spouse and children, at the board meeting and the dinner table. The family in particular is the incubator of civic manners and civic virtues. The kind of people we are—our values, beliefs, and moral sensibilities; what we learn to love and what we learn to loathe—are largely shaped by our families, friends, classmates, and colleagues. We bring those things to politics; that's the stage on which they often play themselves out.

Many years ago a friend told me that if you find yourself overwhelmed by the mess in your room, the best thing to do is to pick up the pile of clothes at your feet. You can't clean up everything at once, but if you clean up the things right in front of you, one at a time, over time the room will become organized and orderly.

The great challenge for a book like this is that its greatest reach may be with people who least need to hear its message. The political entrepreneurs and social provocateurs who win profit and promotion by demeaning politics and coarsening discourse are not going to be swayed by a book like this.

But modern psychology and ancient wisdom both show that the effect of example can be profound. One such example was set by a prophet from Nazareth many years ago, and there have been many since.

Jamil Zaki, director of the Stanford Social Neuroscience Lab, uses tools from psychology and neuroscience to examine empathy, altruism, and social influence. His findings show that witnessing kindness inspires kindness, causing it to spread like a virus. "The battle between dark and light conformity likely depends on which cultural norms people witness most often," he writes.

> Someone who is surrounded by grandstanding and antago-nism will tend towards hostile and exclusionary attitudes herself. Someone who instead learns that her peers prize empathy will put more work to empathize herself, even with people who are different from her. By emphasizing empathy-positive norms, we may be able to leverage the power of social influence to combat apathy and conflict in new ways. And right now, when it comes to mending ideological divides and cultivating kindness, we need every strategy we can find.[54]

If each of us inspires or moves one or two or three other people to give politics—real politics, not just political theater—a second chance, to think twice before sending that inflammatory tweet, or to listen and question instead of jumping to disagree, then there will be millions among us. We don't need to transform everyone's behavior or temperament (something no conservative would ever want to attempt, by the way). Reach the movable middle, and the country and the culture will move with it.

The task of citizenship in America today is not simply to curse the political darkness but to light candles. This can be done one person at a time, in your neighborhood and city, at a homeless shelter and a school board meeting, at neighborhood gatherings and city councils, and in countless other settings. And it can be done starting tomorrow.

What are we waiting for?

CHAPTER 7

The Case for Hope

In 1993 I helped prepare a report, "The Index of Leading Cultural Indicators." Issued by William J. Bennett, it quantified and analyzed social trends over a thirty-year period from 1960 to 1990.

Over the course of those three decades, the United States had indeed experienced substantial social regression. There had been a more than 500 percent increase in violent crime; a more than 400 percent increase in out-of-wedlock births; almost a tripling in the percentage of children on welfare; a tripling of the teenage suicide rate; a doubling of the divorce rate; and a decline of more than seventy points in SAT scores.

The report's conclusion was inescapable: "The forces of social decomposition are challenging—and in some instances overtaking—the forces of social composition."[1]

For my part, I believed that if those trends weren't reversed, they could lead to the decline and maybe even the fall of the republic—and frankly I wasn't all that hopeful that America would turn things around, at least in the short run and absent something like a new religious Great Awakening.

I embraced what at the time was a central conservative tenet: our social problems were linked to a broader cultural collapse, and unless and until we repaired things at the deepest cultural level, we could not really hope to reverse these downward social trends. Culture is upstream from politics, it was (and still is) said; if the culture has decayed, politics can't hope to repair the damage. The report cited the words of Samuel Johnson: "How small, of all that human hearts endure, That part which laws or kings can cause or cure."

But something happened along the road to Gomorrah and the collapse of our culture. Most things started to get better, and many things got much better.

A *Commentary* magazine essay I coauthored in 2007 documented significant progress in the areas of crime and violent crime, drug use, welfare dependency, the rate and total number of abortions, teen sexual activity and births, smoking and binge drinking, and education scores.[2] Surprisingly, the storm clouds, rather than bursting, began to part.

Were we wrong to be so worried about the state of the nation? I don't think so; the negative statistics corresponded to very real instances of human misery and struggle. But many of us underestimated the ability of good governance and the will of the American people to reverse these trends. The improvements were the result of long-overdue changes in both government policy and public attitudes, with each sustaining and feeding the other. One could only come away impressed by the enduring power of policy, properly understood, to influence culture and make things better, often faster than we imagine. There is a reason Americans have traditionally looked to government to solve many of our biggest problems.

THE DESPAIR TEMPTATION

"Isn't he making politics fun again?"

So said Sebastian Gorka about his former boss, President Trump, during a stint as guest host for Salem Radio's Dennis Prager.[3]

Mr. Gorka, the former *Breitbart* editor who worked in the Trump White House for several months as a deputy assistant to the president, was celebrating that Donald Trump was making politics an entertainment show, having moved us away from what he and others considered the staid, tedious, dull politics of previous eras. Discussions about the need to reform entitlement programs and the merits and demerits of a premium support system for Medicare were out; now in were tweets like those attacking Special Counsel Robert Mueller's "WITCH HUNT" and "SPYGATE"; "fake news" networks like CNN and MSNBC, which the president deemed "enemies of the American people"; journalists like "Sleepy Eyes Chuck Todd" of NBC and "Crooked H [Hillary Clinton] flunkie" Maggie Haberman of the *New York Times*; and NFL players kneeling for the national anthem.

The rise of Donald Trump corresponds with the rise, especially on the right, of the politics of performance and theatrics, of drama and melodrama, of reality television and the World Wrestling Federation. Political personalities who not that long ago acted as if they were members of the Congregation of the Doctrine of the Faith—which in the past called for excommunication for any Republican who deviated one iota from what they considered conservative orthodoxy—became utterly bored with policy discussions. For them, Mr. Trump was great for business. Pass the popcorn.

A man utterly indifferent to the craft of governing, Mr. Trump has shown time and time again that he doesn't have even an elementary understanding of his own administration's policies.

One example: in January 2018, the Republican-controlled House was about to vote on legislation to reauthorize the government's authority to conduct foreign surveillance on US soil. The intelligence community considers the program—known as Section 702, named for its place within the Foreign Intelligence Surveillance Amendments Act that established it in 2008—to be its key national security surveillance tool, and the Trump administration had been supportive of it. But the morning of the vote, President Trump saw a segment on *Fox & Friends* disparaging the program and sent out a critical tweet, causing chaos and confusion among Republicans in Congress.

"The president was seemingly misinformed about the nature of the vote and the substance of the bill," according to the *Washington Post*.[4]

Republican support for the program began to crater. Panicked White House aides reached out to Speaker Paul Ryan, who had to walk Mr. Trump through its details. Ninety minutes later, a second tweet was sent out in the president's name walking back the first tweet, this time pushing for the act to be renewed.

According to the *Post*, when President Trump issued his second tweet, House majority leader Kevin McCarthy handed his phone to the bill's sponsor, Intelligence Committee chairman Devin Nunes, who in turn read the tweet aloud to the GOP conference, "calming lawmakers' nerves." (I was told by a high-ranking member of Congress that the second tweet was sent in the president's name but that he was unaware of it. The tweet was actually sent by President Trump's then chief of staff John Kelly.)

The law eventually passed, but what should have been a routine vote was thrown into disarray because the president was clueless about vital legislation supported by his own administration. And this was hardly the first time the president demonstrated such willful ignorance. Friends of former national security advisor H. R. McMaster report that after providing many briefings to President Trump, McMaster concluded that "the guy wasn't absorbing a f***** thing."[5] According to multiple sources, former secretary of state Rex Tillerson referred to Mr. Trump as a "moron."[6] And John Kelly has referred to the president as an "idiot" on multiple occasions, according to several people who claim to have witnessed the comments. (NBC News reported that Kelly portrayed himself to Trump administration aides as "the lone bulwark against catastrophe, curbing the erratic urges of a president who has a questionable grasp on policy issues and the functions of government.")[7]

After a series of meetings and phone calls with high-ranking officials, a Republican who deals regularly with the Trump administration confided in me about his frustration. "The dysfunction in this White House just knows no bounds," he said. At some point that level of dysfunction catches up to the president—and to the country.

That Donald Trump would oversee a dysfunctional White House should have come as news to exactly nobody. But it's not enough to lament that we ended up with a president who is indifferent to governing and unknowledgeable on policy; we need to take a step back and understand *why* such a thing happened.

Much of the explanation is the near-total collapse of trust in the governing class and political establishment.

The most common explanation for this is that the unstated promise to the public was that this elite, if given power, would govern with proficiency, expertise, and skill. The nation would run like a well-oiled machine operated by those who were only too eager to advertise their superior intelligence and ability. But instead, over the last half century we have experienced wars and military interventions gone awry, financial crises, social divisions, and political scandals. They accumulated, one after another, like weights on a scale.

The most significant events were the Vietnam War—not just the failure of the war effort but the lies that accompanied it—and Watergate, a political scandal that brought down an American president. Those were crushing blows from which the federal government has never fully recovered. But there have been many other failings since.[8] From the perspective of the public, these failures melded together into a sweeping, searing indictment of government. Things had gone badly off track, and those in charge were responsible.

National polls have tracked this decline in confidence. Polling evidence shows that trust in the federal government nose-dived from 1965 to 1980. Since then, those numbers have fluctuated, but trust in government is now dramatically below what it was in the middle of the twentieth century. By the 2016 election, we were in the midst of the longest period of low trust in government since the question was first asked in the late 1950s, with no more than about 30 percent having expressed trust in the government in Washington *at any point* over the last decade.[9]

By 2016 we reached an inflection point: only about two in ten Americans trusted the national government, while eight in ten expressed feelings of either frustration or anger with it. Many Americans, furious with the mounting failures and deeply unhappy with the "establishment" candidate (Hillary Clinton), decided it was time to overturn the apple cart. Trust had been breached for long enough. They were mad as hell and weren't going to take it anymore.

The error they made was allowing their disenchantment to overwhelm their good judgment and embrace a fraud. Tens of millions of Americans thought the right response, after giving the middle finger to the establishment, was to first nominate and then elect as president a rank amateur, a businessman who had declared multiple bankruptcies, a person who proudly advertised his ignorance and promised that he could quickly and easily solve the problems facing the country.

This was a failure of citizenship. Instead of demanding more from their elected leaders and more realism from themselves, a lot of Americans went in the opposite direction. They decided the proper response to failure was to promote to the presidency a man who was manifestly unequipped—intellectually, temperamentally, psychologically, and from his life experience—to govern. We now face the task of correcting that mistake, which requires us to rethink things; to reenvision politics and remind ourselves of its deep and true purpose, which is to solve public problems.

THE POPULIST TEMPTATION

As we've seen, trust in government, at least at the federal level, is near all-time lows. And that's not only because of high-profile failures; it's also because much of what government does on a daily basis is inefficient, clumsy, uncoordinated, and wasteful.

In his book *Why Government Fails So Often*, former Yale professor Peter Schuck, a sober, thoughtful scholar on the practice of government—he refers to himself as a "militant moderate"—

argues that *"the federal government does in fact perform poorly in a vast range of domestic programs."*[10] He believes the gap between the goals of government and the amount we spend on it is enormous; that government almost never achieves what it promises; and that the problems are "large, recurrent, and systemic."[11] According to Schuck, "Less than 1 percent of government spending is backed by even the most basic evidence of cost-effectiveness."[12]

Ineffective policies are caused by deep structural factors regardless of which party is in charge, according to Schuck. The administrative state, which is not directly accountable to the citizenry, exercises vast discretionary powers. "The relationship between government's growing ambition and its endemic failure," he writes, "is rooted in an inescapable structural condition: officials' meager tools and limited understanding of the opaque, complex social world that they aim to manipulate." The result is having a corrosive effect on the reputation of government.

National Affairs editor Yuval Levin, in reviewing Schuck's book, highlights a concrete example of a program that performs a vital service but is failing in many important respects: Medicare, the health insurance program for people over sixty-five (and some younger people with disabilities), which accounts for 15 percent of the federal budget and covers almost 60 million Americans:

> By paying a set fee for each service, it creates perverse incentives for doctors to perform more of them. Then, by using the instrument of price controls to limit costs, it creates shortages. By setting those prices administratively, it denies itself the information that only the interplay of supply and demand can offer. By imposing a mid-1960s insurance model on American medicine, it makes the health-care

system inflexible. By relying on payment cuts that Congress routinely puts off, it makes a joke of its own fiscal projections. And by abiding billions in fraud, it invites waste and abuse. The sum of it all is a colossal mess at the heart of American health care.[13]

Schuck points to at least four costs of these government failures: wasted resources and opportunity costs; the indignities people suffer; the dampening effects on economic growth; and undermining the legitimacy of government.

To be successful, public policy needs rigorous measurements, relentless evaluation, and accountability. It has to be adaptable. It needs to put in place the right incentives, simplify rules and administration, and set realistic goals. Wise government sets the circumstances for success while resisting the temptation to centralize power and decision-making. And it needs people in positions of influence who are modest in their expectations, empirical in their approach, and competent in their execution. What government needs, in a word, are professionals. But to repeat: we live in a time when excellence and realism in governing are widely viewed as unimportant, even unfashionable.

Donald Trump understood this far better than anyone else in American politics. Some of the recurrent themes of his rhetoric during the 2016 presidential campaign were that those in power were idiots, the problems facing the United States were simple to fix, and he alone could fix them.

At various points during the campaign he claimed to know more than anyone on earth—and sometimes more than anyone in American history—about tax laws, banking, money, renewable energy, the debt, the visa system, trade, jobs, infrastructure, the military, ISIS, the horror of nuclear war, campaign contributions, and our system of government.[14] This despite the fact that Mr. Trump had no previous experience in many of these areas, and frankly knew nothing about them.

At one point near the end of the campaign, Mr. Trump declared, "Together we're going to deliver real change that once again puts Americans first. That begins with immediately repealing and replacing the disaster known as Obamacare. . . . You're going to have such great health care, at a tiny fraction of the cost—and it's going to be so easy."

But as president, Mr. Trump failed to repeal and replace Obamacare—and in a meeting with the nation's governors in February 2017, he admitted, "Now, I have to tell you, it's an unbelievably complex subject. Nobody knew health care could be so complicated." In fact, *everyone* who has ever delved into healthcare policy knows it is an enormously complicated subject. Donald Trump assumed it was easy to deal with in part because he had apparently never given a moment's thought to it.

But there was more to it than that. Mr. Trump's critiques were laced with contempt for the political establishment and policy experts because he was effectively tapping into a populist spirit that is sweeping much of the Western world.

There are numerous reasons for the rise of populism. According to William Galston, a political theorist who was a domestic-policy advisor in the Bill Clinton White House, they include uneven prosperity and widening income inequality, the erosion of the manufacturing sector and the "urbanization of opportunity," and the fallout from the Great Recession of 2008. These economic factors were combined with the inability of many Western governments to deal with waves of immigration in ways that commanded public support, and with widening cultural divisions between those with college degrees and those without them.[15] The result is a backlash that has disrupted the post–World War II bargain between elites and citizens.

It should be said that populism can be, in limited doses, an understandable response to massive and rapid economic and social changes, and it can even offer useful correctives. It can alert elites to problems to which they may be oblivious.

Most populists start with a legitimate issue or grievance, but the danger lies in excessively stirring emotions and passions to gain support, thus sowing cynicism and mistrust. Such was the case with William Jennings Bryan, who, in the 1896 "Cross of Gold" speech that won him the Democratic nomination, argued for an "easy money" policy in response to the depressed economy at the time. Bryan advocated changing the nation's monetary backing from gold to silver. "Great cities," Bryan said in his defense of farmers, "rest upon our broad and fertile prairies. Burn down your cities and leave our farms, and your cities will spring up again as if by magic; but destroy our farms, and the grass will grow in the streets of every city in the country." Bryan saw it as his mission to protect the most vulnerable Americans from the damages caused by industrialization and went after what he called "the money power," but he ended up exacerbating divisions in the country.

In its more extreme form, populism "pits a virtuous and homogeneous people against a set of elites and dangerous 'others' who are together depicted as depriving (or attempting to deprive) the sovereign people of their rights, values, prosperity, identity

and voice."[16] Unhealthy populism is defined by a sense of grievance and resentment, which is why it's a mode of politics that has
historically been susceptible to demagogues.

Among the most notable examples of a populist American
demagogue is George Wallace, the aggressively segregation-
ist governor of Alabama who ran for president in 1968 as the
head of the American Independent Party. (Wallace carried five
southern states—Alabama, Arkansas, Georgia, Louisiana, and
Mississippi—and won forty-six electoral votes.) Wallace railed
against, among others, Hippies, Vietnam War protesters, "welfare loafers," foreign aid, arrogant judges, cowardly politicians,
and "pointy-head college professors who can't even park a bicycle
straight." During that campaign Wallace, doing his part for civility in public discourse, declared, "Hell, we got too much dignity
in government now, what we need is some meanness."

In his book *Wallace*, Marshall Frady wrote, "There is something primordially exciting and enthralling about him." Frady
added, "As long as we are creatures hung halfway between the
cave and the stars, figures like Wallace can be said to pose the
great dark original threat," with "the potential for an American
fascism."[17]

Wallace's daughter, Peggy Wallace Kennedy, said of Wallace
and Trump, "They both were able to adopt the notion that fear
and hate are the two greatest motivators of voters that feel alienated from government."[18]

Populism also needs enemies, lots of them, and especially
elites who—the narrative goes—are selfish, greedy, insulated,
and power-hungry. The out-of-touch elites are viewed as enemies
of the people, and they need to be treated as such.

Excoriating elites "is classic populist language," according to

Yale historian Beverly Gage. "Trump has taken it to a whole new level by not only attacking clueless elites but the entire idea of expertise."[19]

The result is this: many Americans are drenched in a distaste for the actual practice of politics, and among activists in the Republican Party in particular there is an unspoken sense that the activity of governing is somehow illegitimate. This is one of the fundamental differences between the American Right today and the conservative movement that shaped me. It helps explain how Mr. Trump seized on deeply antipolitical feelings and leveraged them to his advantage, why Republicans so devalued any focus on policy during the 2016 election, and why Mr. Trump was not penalized but rewarded for his vast ignorance on matters of public policy.

During the 2016 primary I could not understand how it was that a man who in debate after debate proved he couldn't string together three coherent policy sentences kept getting stronger rather than weaker. The answer is that such an approach can only work with people who disdain the craft of governing. They were looking for "outsiders" who gave voice to their frustration and rage, even if they had never governed in their lives. Remember, they were (and are) operating on the assumption that governing is simple, lawmakers are fools and knaves, and the system is thoroughly and endemically corrupt. The federal government is "the swamp," while the political class and civil servants are part of the "deep state." The system is "rigged." As a result the village needs to be (figuratively) burned to the ground. Donald Trump was the appointed arsonist.

At the risk of being accused of being an elitist, I believe this attitude is wildly misguided and naive. As I've already argued, in many respects government, especially at the federal level, is performing poorly. It is often antiquated, unresponsive, and failing to meet the needs of the citizenry. The unhappiness with government is therefore understandable and to some degree justified.

But the solution isn't to elect people who are inexperienced, inept, and contemptuous of governing.

THE DELICATE ART OF SOLVING NATIONAL PROBLEMS

The founders articulated the aims of government in the preamble to the Constitution:

> We the People of the United States, in Order to form a more perfect Union, establish Justice, insure domestic Tranquility, provide for the common defence, promote the general Welfare, and secure the Blessings of Liberty to ourselves and our Posterity, do ordain and establish this Constitution for the United States of America.

The purpose of the Constitution, then, was to create an effective national government that would meet the needs and protect the rights of the people in ways they can't do by themselves. That has always mattered, but it's particularly relevant now, since, as William J. Bennett and John J. DiIulio Jr. have written, "virtually every aspect of our lives is now touched by government."[20]

They list some of the activities, including underwriting support for the elderly and disabled, for medical research, space missions, art museums, farmers, and mass transit. The federal government subsidizes public television. It builds prisons and supports public-housing projects. It provides food stamps, health care, college scholarships, loans, and grants. It involves itself in university admissions, hiring practices, family-leave policies, civil-rights laws, banking insurance and regulation, professional accrediting, air-traffic control, and parks administration. It protects our air, water, and food; regulates tobacco and automobiles; constructs interstate highways; keeps out illegal immigrants; and provides pensions to our veterans. And of course it funds the military.

Many people, particularly on the right, believe the federal government is a modern-day Leviathan—unwieldy and inherently ineffective, its size, reach, and cost ($4 trillion and counting) completely out of control, and in possession of unprecedented and unconstitutional power. The government is profoundly mistrusted, they argue, and it's time for it to be pulled up root and branch.

There are some parts of this critique I'm sympathetic to, but the simple fact is that there is no evidence the public wants anything like a large-scale rollback of the federal government. Time after time, in election after election, voters have shown that they are basically happy with the *domains* in which government is acting and prepared to defend the existence of programs that were created in the wake of the New Deal and the Great Society, if not always their performance.

Republicans have now and then made an effort to cut the size and cost of government in significant ways but rarely with success. That is true even of Ronald Reagan, who was the most ideologically conservative president in modern times and the one most rhetorically committed to cutting government. "In this present crisis, government is not the solution to our problem; government is the problem," Reagan said in his first inaugural address.

The reality is that Reagan, contrary to the claims of some of his conservative admirers, did not roll back government to anything like the extent he promised. Indeed, especially after his first year in the presidency, he devoted most of his energies elsewhere. Thus, although at first approving a plan to cut Social Security benefits for prospective early retirees, he quickly capitulated and scrapped the idea. Nor did he ever mount a serious effort to reform the structural design of other entitlement programs. In fact, Reagan enacted what at the time was the most dramatic expansion of Medicare coverage since its inception, including a complex system of price controls. And he not only didn't eliminate any cabinet departments but rather added to them. During his presidency, federal spending as a percent of GDP was higher than it was under Jimmy Carter. Under Reagan, the national debt skyrocketed. Like most conservatives, Reagan opposed Big Government in the abstract more than he did in the particulars.

There is no doubt that overall Reagan would have preferred to cut government more, but there was no public will for it, and to move adamantly on this front would have forced him to forgo other, more achievable goals, such as deregulation, cutting tax rates, and building up the military.

Most people have forgotten something else Reagan said in his first inaugural address: "Now, so there will be no misunderstanding, it's not my intention to do away with government. It is rather to make it work—work with us, not over us; to stand by our side, not ride on our back. Government can and must provide opportunity, not smother it; foster productivity, not stifle it."

Reagan was a conservative, not an anarchist. Unlike too many of the people who call themselves conservatives today, he sought to limit government in order to strengthen its legitimacy—not to disrupt or discredit it.

Conservatives have fallen lately into the trap of believing that the essential question when it comes to governing is how big the government is or how much it spends. But at least as important is what it does and how it works. The trouble with this question is that it requires real engagement with the details of governing and of public policy. And ultimately, to take politics seriously, we will need just such engagement.

Nearly all of the actual policy achievements of the right in the modern era tend to support this point, even if conservatives are inclined to ignore them. In fact, we have seen time and again that when conservatives engage with the political process, they use their principles to make headway against some of our toughest problems.

Let's start with welfare. The 1996 welfare law (championed by conservatives and signed into law by President Clinton) reversed sixty years of federal policy by ending welfare as an entitlement program. It imposed a five-year time limit on the receipt of benefits, required a large percentage of recipients to seek and obtain work, and enhanced enforcement of child support.

Despite predictions of catastrophic damage to the poor, the results were astonishing. Within half a decade, the national welfare caseload declined by almost 60 percent while employment figures for single mothers rose and overall poverty, child poverty (including among African American children), and child hunger decreased.

What's less well known is that the shift from the old welfare system (Aid to Families with Dependent Children) to the new system (Temporary Assistance for Needy Families) initially cost *more* money. But the point of welfare reform wasn't just to cut spending; it was to reform a program that was poorly serving those it was intended to help. This required government to realign rewards and penalties.

It's the same story with crime. The violent crime rate has been cut roughly in half since 1993, with the homicide and robbery rates each having fallen by more than 50 percent. The drop in crime was not a result of smaller government; it was a result of better and smarter government, including more incarceration, elevated security, better intervention and prevention programs, an increase in police officers per capita, enforcing quality-of-life offenses, more effective identification of criminal patterns, and more advanced use of data. (Unlike welfare, where the federal government instituted reforms, in the case of crime most of the reforms were undertaken by state and local governments.)

A third major policy success is the earned-income tax credit. Created during the Ford presidency, it is a federal tax credit for low- and moderate-income working people. It was expanded under Presidents Reagan, Clinton, George W. Bush, and Obama. The program has lifted around 6 million people above the poverty line and reduced the severity of poverty for more than 18 million people.[21] While costing the government more than $60 billion per year, the earned-income tax credit is perhaps the best antipoverty program we have. "No other tax or transfer program prevents more children from living a life of poverty," according to an analysis by the Brookings Institution, "and only Social Security keeps more people above poverty."[22]

There have been other successes of a conservative variety, from tax reform and deregulation in the 1980s to the antidrug efforts in the early 1990s to the charter school movement and the greater market competition introduced into Medicare in the 2000s.

These reforms shared a rigorous empirical approach. They took into account the fact that people are free and independent yet also act in their self-interest and respond to incentives. They were open to experimentation and adjustment. They measured success by outcomes rather than inputs. And they rejected what Reagan called a "slavish adherence to abstraction" in favor of a commitment to actual achievement. They were driven not by ceaseless hostility to government but by a restrained, realistic vision of its potential.

There are, of course, countless examples of the good that government at every level (local, state, and federal) has done in people's lives—mandating vaccinations for preventable childhood diseases, allowing people to walk city streets in safety, ensuring the air we breathe and water we drink is safe, paving roads that allow us to travel and engage in commerce, overseeing civil aviation that allows us to fly safely from one coast to the other, defending us from foreign enemies, and much more—and most of us take for granted the ways government, however imperfect, works and has allowed us to go about our lives.

Even if one looks objectively at the noted political failures mentioned earlier, one could argue that this perspective reflects a glass-half-empty perspective by ignoring what government has accomplished:

- America lost the Vietnam War—but it also won the Cold War.
- Watergate was an example of widespread political corruption—but our institutions held up, the rule of law prevailed, and Richard Nixon resigned.

- The financial system did collapse in 2008—but those in power acted in a way that averted a second Great Depression. What followed is one of the longest economic expansions on record.
- College tuition is exorbitant—but America also has the finest system of higher education in the world.
- Our world is getting hotter and the oceans are rising— but in the United States our water and air are much cleaner than they were several decades ago.
- There are still far too many mass killings in America— but violent crime is dramatically lower today than it was a quarter century ago.
- Our entitlement system hasn't been modernized and is far too costly—but providing financial security to and virtually eliminating poverty among the elderly is a great achievement.
- Not enough has been done to contain the opioid epidemic—but among the most important successes over the last half century has been a substantial reduction in smoking rates in the general population.

Let's stipulate, then, that there have been more failures than there should have been and certainly many more failures than the public had been conditioned to expect. But let's remember, too, that we cannot make perfection the price of confidence in government. We need to have higher standards, and we need to have reasonable expectations. Right now we're both aiming too low and expecting too much. And we need to recognize that when government functions well, people tend not to give it a second thought.

LESSONS FROM THE TRENCHES

Because politics is designed to solve our problems and has done so throughout our history, we can't afford to let despair drive our choices in politicians. Instead, we should be spurred to put a higher premium on politicians who demonstrate competence and creativity, experience and artistry, wisdom and sound judgment. We need more people with those qualities, not fewer of them.

We need such individuals because it turns out it isn't all that easy to govern well. Doing so is a good deal harder task than most people might appreciate, and it's certainly harder than giving speeches and issuing ten-point plans; than writing op-eds, hosting a radio talk show, or sitting around the kitchen table dispensing advice on curbing gun violence, reversing global warming, reducing out-of-wedlock births, ending the Syrian civil war, or brokering peace between Israel and the Palestinians. It's also much easier to criticize those in government than it is to sympathize with the challenges they face.

Having spent around a dozen years in three administrations, having served in two federal agencies (the Department of Education and the Office of National Drug Control Policy) and as a senior advisor in the White House, there are certain impressions and lessons I've come away with, some of which have been learned the hard way, through trial and error.

They are impressions and lessons consistent with the experience of others, Democrats and Republicans, who have served in high public office. And they hopefully provide a more detailed and accurate picture of what life in politics and the White House is like, what some of the challenges are, and what might be done to improve the chances of success. Responsible citizenship entails doing certain things as individuals, but it also involves showing some empathy for the challenges faced by those who hold positions of power. "For half a century," Raymond Aron wrote, "I have limited my freedom of criticism by asking the question: In his place, what would I do?"[23]

This begins by recognizing that, particularly when it comes to life in the White House, some days will be better than others, but no days are uncomplicated or effortless. As President Eisenhower told his successor, John F. Kennedy, the day before Kennedy was sworn in, "There are no easy matters that will ever come to you as president. If they are easy, they will be settled at a lower level."

When people run for public office, they tend to present the choices facing America in Manichean terms. Politics is often framed as a zero-sum game, with all the arguments lining up on your (and your supporters') side and none on the other, and once you arrive at the right solution—once you check the right policy box—the hard work is done. All you need after that is for Congress to pass legislation, that it be quickly and efficiently implemented, and all will be right with the world.

It turns out that governing is a good deal more complicated. "There are few things wholly evil or wholly good," Lincoln said. "Almost everything, especially of government policy, is an inseparable compound of the two, so that our best judgment of the preponderance between them is continually demanded."

In my experience, when debating the merits of certain public policies, you'll often hear competing arguments made by knowledgeable, articulate individuals that sound convincing. Both sides usually make valid points—and usually have weaknesses. One policy may improve things in a certain area; another policy may improve things in a different area.

For example, tax cuts may increase economic growth while increasing the deficit and widening income inequality. Imposing steel quotas may protect the steel industry, but as a result steel is more expensive for automakers, a cost that is passed on to consumers and places the US automotive industry at a competitive disadvantage. So steps that may help one sector may hurt another. Mandatory minimum sentencing laws may decrease crime by keeping some very bad people in prison for a very long time—but their effects may not be as great as many people think, and they might also put too many people behind bars who shouldn't be there, which can have a devastating impact on communities and families.

In 1994 Bill Clinton decided against intervening in the Rwandan civil war, in part because the United States had just pulled American troops out of a disastrous peacekeeping mission in Somalia. The Clinton administration vowed it would never again intervene in a conflict involving clan and tribal conflicts it didn't fully understand in a nation where the United States had no obvious national interests. That was an understandable reaction, but it came at a huge humanitarian cost. Bill Clinton has since called his failure to intervene in Rwanda one of his biggest regrets, saying that he believes had the US intervened, even marginally, at the beginning of the genocide, at least 300,000 people might have been saved.[24]

Case Study: The Iraq War

It would be impossible for me to speak of such difficult judgments in our recent past without taking up the Iraq War, which began in 2003 under the leadership of the Bush administration, in which I served as a senior official.

It can be difficult to recall now, but the decision to launch the war in Iraq won overwhelming support in Congress (the vote was 296–133 in the House and 77–23 in the Senate) and had the overwhelming backing of the American people (72 percent).

It is important to remember, too, that the administration's determination to act was rooted in the view, shared by the governments of virtually the entire world, including intelligence agencies of nations that opposed the war, that Saddam Hussein possessed weapons of mass destruction (WMD). Not only did the intelligence community (IC) believe this, but their findings were reinforced by the fact that Saddam had used them in the past, had admitted to possessing WMD in the mid-1990s, and was impeding UN inspections. We were also aware that US intelligence had *underestimated* how close Saddam was to acquiring WMD prior to the 1991 Gulf War.

In addition, the official policy of the US government was regime change—a policy put into place not by George W. Bush but by Bill Clinton. The reason was that Saddam's regime was genocidal, destabilizing, and aggressive (Saddam had started a war with Iran, invaded Kuwait, and attacked Israel with ballistic missiles). The sanctions regimen against Iraq was crumbling. And President Bush won support for a UN Security Council resolution demanding full Iraqi compliance with inspections, a final chance to come clean before war commenced. (Resolution 1441 found Iraq in "material breach" of its obligations to disarm and warned of "severe consequences" if it did not comply. Saddam refused.)

All of this was, of course, taking place in the shadow of the attacks on September 11, 2001. It wasn't simply that those attacks shifted the risk assessment calculus of President Bush, convincing him that Saddam with WMD was a threat we could not tolerate in a post-9/11 world; the president also believed there was a moral case to liberate Iraq and the region from a genocidal dictator. (Prior to the war, Elie Wiesel, the author, Holocaust survivor, and Nobel Peace Prize recipient, told President Bush, "Mr. President, you have a moral obligation to act against evil.") If Saddam was removed from power, the immediate question would become this: What kind of government should Iraq have instead? President Bush decided the best option would be to support a new regime that was democratic and respected human rights and the rule of law.

We believed, then, that a toxic confluence of factors converged on Saddam and his regime: malevolence, aggression, a fondness for terrorists, hatred for America, an insatiable appetite for weapons of mass murder, and a willingness to use them, on his own people and on other people.

And so at 10:16 p.m. eastern time on March 19, 2003, after repeated efforts to persuade Saddam to open up his regime to international inspections had failed, President Bush announced, "My fellow citizens, at this hour, American and coalition forces are in the early stages of military operations to disarm Iraq, to free its people, and to defend the world from grave danger."

We all know the rest of the story: The president and those of us who worked in his administration believed Saddam Hussein had WMD, but it turned out he did not. As the bipartisan Silberman-Robb Commission report stated, "We conclude that the Intelligence Community was dead wrong in almost all of its pre-war judgments about Iraq's weapons of mass destruction. This was a major intelligence failure."[25] And it was a failure on our part in not probing the evidence more deeply.

Making matters worse, the occupation strategy following

Saddam's overthrow was badly flawed. We opted for a "light foot-print" approach to avoid being seen as an occupying power, when in fact what was needed was a far larger American military presence to keep Iraq from descending into chaos and even civil war, which eventually became the case. The goal was to quickly hand over responsibility to the Iraqis and an international stabilizing force; instead, an insurgency arose, and for three-and-a-half years Iraq was beset by violence, instability, terrorism, and murderous sectarian strife.

In 2007—with a weary public wanting to give up on the war effort and facing threats of defections in his own party—President Bush jettisoned the failing "light footprint" approach and embraced the so-called surge strategy that turned the war around. Even President Obama admitted as much in 2011, when he said, "We're leaving behind a sovereign, stable and self-reliant Iraq, with a representative government that was elected by its people." This was, he said, a "moment of success."[26] The surge was one of the most impressive and politically courageous decisions I've witnessed in politics. Yet that success was undone when President Obama, against the advice of his military commanders and the pleas of many Iraqi leaders, withdrew all US forces from Iraq, allowing terrorist groups there to reconstitute themselves.

My point in raising the Iraq War isn't to justify it; in retrospect the war was clearly a mistake, and if I knew then what I came to know later, I would have opposed it. Nor am I offering excuses for the administration in which I served. The errors in judgment and execution we made were grave.

Rather, I want to remind people who may have forgotten that it was by no means an easy call. At the time there seemed to be a plausible rationale for going to war, which is why it had the widespread support it did. Nor was it the case that we didn't consider the arguments against the war. In fact, I laid out—in a September 17, 2002, White House document—the strongest case against our policy on Iraq, consisting of thirteen specific arguments. For example:

- "Going to war with Iraq will almost by definition divert attention and resources from the pursuit of al Qaeda. And it was al Qaeda, not Iraq, that killed more than 3,000 of our countrymen."
- "What will a post-Saddam Iraq look like? How long will we stay? How much are we willing to spend?"
- "Saddam may be malevolent—but he's not suicidal. Everyone knows he's not going to attack America because everyone knows that if he does, it will lead to the incineration of his nation. Nor is he stupid enough to use terrorist networks to do his dirty deeds. His aim is arguably to control the gulf region; it's not to send nuclear bombs to Manhattan. By the way, what *is* the evidence that Iraq is preparing to launch an attack on the United States? You can't show me any, because there is none. We know three relevant facts, all of which work against your case: first, Saddam does not have a nuclear weapon; second, if he gets them, he doesn't have the means to deliver them to America; and third, there's no proof whatsoever that he intends to attack America. It's based purely on speculation, which is a thin reed on which to base a war decision."

To be clear, I supported our policy at the time, I believed the war was justified, and I publicly defended it. We believed the arguments for war outweighed the arguments against it. Yet it wasn't as if we didn't consider the downsides of the war. We did. But we made wrong judgments, which came àt a terrible price.

FINDING HOPE IN THE DARK

The eighteenth-century British statesman Edmund Burke wrote to a friend and fellow member of Parliament acknowledging, "Every political question I have ever known has had so much of the pro and con in it that nothing but the success could decide which proposition was to have been adopted."[27]

Burke was right. It's impossible to know the exact consequences once abstract ideas are (imperfectly) put into effect in the real world, which is untidy and unpredictable. Building highways is one thing; changing human behavior is quite another.

The pioneering computer engineer and systems scientist Jay Forrester explained that we learn to think in simple loop systems, while social problems arise out of complex systems. What makes sense for one doesn't work for the other. "With a high degree of confidence we can say that the intuitive solution to the problems of complex social systems will be wrong most of the time," according to Forrester.[28]

It doesn't help, of course, that there is very little time to step back, to reflect and ruminate, for those in positions of power. The crush of events is simply too much, with deadlines sometimes forcing decisions that have not been fully thought through.

In the early years of the Reagan presidency, the director of the Office of Management and Budget, David Stockman, was the point person of the so-called Reagan Revolution, an effort to frontally assault the American welfare state. (Stockman failed in his attempt.) Stockman—young, bright, highly knowledgeable, and highly ambitious—was the central figure for the administration on domestic and economic policy. In interviews with a journalist at *The Atlantic*, Stockman allowed the public to peek behind the curtain and see how chaotic policy making can be.

"I just wish that there were more hours in the day or that we didn't have to do this so fast," Stockman told William Greider in 1981. "I have these stacks of briefing books and I've got to make decisions about specific options. . . . I don't have time, trying to put this whole package together in three weeks, so you just start making snap judgments."[29]

He added, "I'm sort of into a permanent mobilization. I just go home and sleep for a few hours and come back and start pushing. I'll philosophize about it afterwards. I can't do it now. I've just got to keep moving." [30]

The result? "None of us really understands what's going on with all these numbers," confessed Stockman, the one person who *should* have understood what was going on with all those numbers. "You've got so many different budgets out and so many different baselines and such complexity now in the interactive parts of the budget between policy action and the economic environment and all the internal mysteries of the budget, and there are a lot of them. People are getting from A to B and it's not clear how they are getting there."[31]

Those in decision-making positions, then, are often forced to make consequential decisions on incomplete information in a compressed period of time in order to solve difficult and enduring problems. And the outcome of those decisions may well be determined by contingencies you cannot anticipate.

Politicians are like everyone else; they want to control events rather than to be at their mercy. But sometimes "life is a theater of vicissitudes," as John Adams put it. Presidents have a set of expectations on how their tenure will unfold, but events may well intervene.

John F. Kennedy faced unanticipated crises in Cuba and Berlin. George W. Bush's presidency was transformed by the attacks on September 11, 2001. Barack Obama inherited a titanic financial crisis that occurred just before the 2008 election. None of these men could have known what lay ahead, and events forced them to adjust their priorities, to immerse themselves in matters they might have preferred to ignore. But sometimes that's not an option.

Confounding matters even more is a great paradox at the heart of the presidency. It is, to be sure, the most powerful office in the world. But to assume events can be shaped like hot wax sets presidents and their advisors up for an endless series of frustrations. From the outset it's important to recognize that constraints on one's ability to shape events are far greater than most people imagine.

As president, the capacity to *shape* public opinion is considerable, while the capacity to *change* public opinion is less than you may think. Presidential scholars like George C. Edwards III have shown that the essence of successful presidential leadership is recognizing and exploiting existing opportunities, not creating them through persuasion. Edwards makes a strong case that to avoid overreaching, presidents should be alert to the limitations on their power to persuade and rigorously assess the possibilities for obtaining public and congressional support in their environments.

"A statesman who too far outruns the experience of his people will fail in achieving domestic consensus, however wise his policies," Henry Kissinger wrote in his book, *A World Restored*.[32] In addition, overpromising is a staple of campaigns; politicians believe that to be elected, they have to make extravagant claims. But former Nixon speechwriter William Safire warned that the politicians who promise the rain are held responsible for the drought. And droughts will come.

THE UNDERAPPRECIATED VIRTUE OF DISCERNMENT

Effective governing requires having the right principles and deciding on the right policy; but it also necessitates *discernment*, the ability to apply principles to particular issues in particular circumstances. Is it the right time to push a far-reaching reform of, say, an entitlement program? Is the country ready for it? Is your party? What are the odds of success? What are the opportunity costs of failure? Will other items on your agenda suffer because of it? Those are all considerations that need to be factored in.

Some examples from my own experience: In the first months of his first term, George W. Bush championed education reform (No Child Left Behind) and tax cuts. These were issues he had run on during the campaign, so they didn't come as a surprise to anyone, and a president's first year is usually the most productive one when it comes to the implementation of his agenda. By the summer of 2001, we had secured passage of both. Two years later, President Bush signed into law landmark Medicare reform legislation that included a prescription drug benefit, more choices for older Americans, and more control over their health care.

At the outset of George W. Bush's second term, however, we decided to make a big push for reforming Social Security, including giving younger workers the option of directing some of their

Social Security tax payments into a personal account that could be invested in broadly based index funds. (Those who were retired or nearing retirement would have seen little change.)

I believed then, and I believe now, it was a needed change. But the public (and therefore Congress) didn't agree, and even after months of concentrated effort, we weren't even able to get a bill out of committee, let alone get a vote on the floor of the House and Senate. As a result of going with Social Security as our first initiative in the second term, we had to delay immigration and health-care reform. By the time we got around to those, the moment was lost, and we fell just short of the votes needed for passage of immigration reform and couldn't even get Congress to notice Bush's health-care proposals. Had we gone with immigration ahead of Social Security, we might well have secured passage of a far-reaching and necessary reform. But because of the sequencing, neither reform saw the light of day. It's clear in retrospect what our mistake was, but at the time there were strong arguments for what we chose to do.

Successful governing, then, requires prescience and discipline when it comes to both choosing and pushing an agenda, since so many issues vie for attention. It also requires an excellent staff, and that is not as easy to obtain as one might think.

Staffing a White House isn't simply a matter of assembling intelligent, accomplished people. It's also important that at least some number of them be people of good character, wise judgment, and who get along well with others. Staffing a White House with senior advisors who are brilliant but abrasive, difficult personalities can lead to dysfunction, backbiting, and chaos.

An example: For the first part of the George H. W. Bush presidency, the two most important figures on the staff were John

Sununu and Richard Darman. They were men of deep knowledge but also prickly and imperious. Sununu was eventually fired; Darman managed to stay on. The staff itself—at least on the political and domestic policy side of things—never jelled, and it was costly. (The foreign policy team ran unusually smoothly.)

In the Reagan presidency, Donald Regan—who had had a successful career as chairman and CEO of Merrill Lynch and was an able secretary of the treasury in the first term—turned out to be a disastrous chief of staff in Reagan's second term, alienating, among others, First Lady Nancy Reagan. (She described Regan as "explosive and difficult to deal with.")

But playing well with others hardly exhausts the list of qualities one needs to look for in a staff. It's important to have aides who are willing to challenge prevailing assumptions and group think, who will cross-examine what's being said. It was said of Richard Helms, CIA director under Nixon, that he never hesitated to warn the White House of dangers, even when his views ran counter to the preconceptions of the president or of his security advisor.

When I moved from deputy director of presidential speechwriting to head of the Office of Strategic Initiatives (OSI), I detailed in a memorandum how I envisioned the job. One element involved what I termed playing devil's advocate.

"I've found it useful from time to time," I wrote, "to prepare memoranda that anticipate (and effectively summarize) the strongest case *against* our position on an important issue—and then respond to it." My experience, I added, "is that this exercise helps to clarify and refine thinking. It can help us to better defend ourselves, intellectually and politically. And once in a while it may highlight weaknesses in our own position, so we can adjust it if necessary."

I went on to say, "On certain key issues, I have found it useful to analyze them carefully and thoroughly—and in some cases, I have engaged in a back-and-forth, a *sic et non* [yes and no], in the same memorandum." I did that on several issues, including a long document in the summer of 2001 stating the case for and against embryonic stem cell research, which helped form the basis of President Bush's first prime-time speech, announcing his policy on embryonic stem cell research. If I had to do it over again, I'd do this kind of thing more often, on more issues. I would press, and press again, and press a third time.

THE NEED FOR TRUTH TELLERS

It also helps to have people around a president who have the courage to tell him when he's wrong, who will convey bad news in unvarnished ways, and who refuse to indulge his worst instincts.

One of the reasons for the fall of Richard Nixon is that he didn't have enough people around him who challenged his paranoia, his petty resentments and insecurity, his get-even mindset. Watergate had its roots in the sense of being under siege and in the "us-versus-them" mentality that existed in the Nixon White House.

Charles Colson, who was a senior political advisor to Nixon, described in a 1992 interview what it was like on election night 1972, when Richard Nixon won the largest landslide in American history. President Nixon watched the returns with Colson and the White House chief of staff, H. R. Haldeman. "I couldn't feel any sense of jubilation," Colson admitted. "Here we were, supposedly winning, and it was more like we'd lost."

"The attitude was, 'Well, we showed them, we got even with

our enemies and we beat them,' instead of 'We've been given a wonderful mandate to rule over the next four years,'" Colson said. "We were reduced to our petty worst on the night of what should have been our greatest triumph."[33] Nixon needed people to check his most destructive qualities; in many cases, however, he surrounded himself with people who accentuated them.

Yet the task of governing well doesn't end with embracing wise policies and having a first-rate staff. There is still the need to build a political coalition that can turn good ideas into actual laws. To get legislation passed requires trade-offs, wheeling and dealing, and backroom agreements. Barack Obama ran for president in 2008 promising that lobbyists and special interests would be banned from influencing legislation—but when crunch time came and he needed to secure the votes for passage of the Affordable Care Act (aka Obamacare), drug industry lobbyists worked with Democratic staffers to write the bill.[34]

Certain provisions may be added to a bill that are important to win support of key members of Congress—provisions that might help the constituents in those members' districts (whom the member is elected to represent, after all) but might also make the bill in question more costly. It may look to all the world like a legal buy-off for a vote—"If you vote with us, you'll get money appropriated to build that highway in your district or fund that community health center or public works project you've been asking for." The provision itself may not be defensible—but supporting it *might* well be defensible to get a good, if imperfect, bill turned into law.

Even if one is able to build a successful coalition, however, the work is *still* not yet done. There remains the challenge of gaining control over the permanent bureaucracy that is responsible for carrying out policy, which even the most adept presidents have found difficult to contend with. The permanent bureaucracy is filled with career public servants, many of whom are quite able but are also wedded to the status quo, often risk averse and resistant to change, and skilled at creating roadblocks when it comes to implementation. Translating policies into action, then, isn't easy; there are countless ways civil servants can impede the agenda of presidents, cabinet members, and members of Congress.

Daniel Patrick Moynihan was one of the extraordinary figures in modern American politics. A lifelong Democrat, he served in the administrations of Presidents Kennedy, Johnson, Nixon, and Ford, was ambassador to India and the United Nations, and represented New York in the US Senate for four terms. Moynihan was also an intellectual of the first rank.

In writing about the Great Society, which he was largely sympathetic to, Moynihan wrote, "One of the anomalies of the 1960's is that a period of such extraordinary effort at social improvement should have concluded in a miasma, some would say a maelstrom, of social dissatisfaction." He added:

> During the 1960's a quite extraordinary commitment was made by the national government to put an end to poverty. Yet the effort to do so went forward in entirely too fragmented a manner. In effect, a collection of programs was put together and it was hoped these would somehow add up to a policy. I don't believe they did.[35]

It was not because of lack of effort or good intentions. Nor were the architects of this massive undertaking unintelligent; quite the opposite. Many of them were highly accomplished. But as I've tried to show, governing can be hard, the problems law-makers are trying to solve are often complex and intractable, and the consequences of one set of actions may result in an entirely new set of problems.

This isn't an argument for throwing up our hands in despair; it's an argument for understanding that the case for politics needs to have at its very core the case for policy and problem solving. The job of politics is inseparable from the job of governing, and if we treat our politics as theater, then our government will degen-erate into theater.

I understand that the theatrical and performative side of pol-itics is easier—that it is easier to treat issues like immigration, crime, abortion, race, welfare, and religious liberties as part of a broader ideological war than as problems to be thoughtfully addressed—but in the end, treating politics as a form of self-expression derails the serious work of governing. And that work can save millions of lives.

In 2003 President George W. Bush proposed, and Congress passed, a $15 billion initiative to fight the HIV/AIDS epidemic in Africa. (At the time the projections were that if left unchecked, the disease would kill 68 million people by 2020.) It constituted the largest international health initiative ever to combat a specific disease. "I hoped it would serve as a medical version of the Mar-shall Plan," Bush has written.[36]

It did, and it didn't happen by accident. It was the product of the president's personal commitment, the clear goals he laid out and his insistence that we be extremely ambitious, and a White House policy process that worked superbly well. It was overseen by Josh Bolten, then deputy chief of staff to the president and one of the most able individuals I have ever worked with; and it

involved experts in infectious diseases and international development, the director of national AIDS policy, and top staffers from
the National Security Council and the Office of Management
and Budget.

When President Bush announced the initiative in his 2003
State of the Union address, he said, "Seldom has history offered a
greater opportunity to do so much for so many."

There was no domestic political payoff to the global AIDS initiative. But it was a work of mercy, and by the time Bush left office
in January 2009, the global AIDS initiative supported treatment
for more than 2 million people and care for more than 10 million.
More than 15 million mothers and babies were protected, and
nearly 60 million people had benefited from AIDS testing and
counseling sessions. Africans referred to it as the Lazarus Effect,
after the friend of Jesus who was raised from the dead.[37]

CHOOSING CITIZENSHIP OVER CYNICISM

Immediately before I served in the Reagan, George H. W. Bush,
and George W. Bush administrations, and immediately after I
left them, my IQ was about thirty points higher. Or so it seemed.

The explanation is simple: I *left* government and began to critique those who serve *in* government. It turns out that offering
opinions in a *New York Times* column, on television, or from behind a microphone is a lot easier than actually governing. Like
the rest of the world, I can watch Republicans and Democrats
serving in government and, from a safe distance after things have
played out, explain how things could have been done so much
better and so much easier. And I can do so in nine hundred words
or in five minutes on television.

The difference between governing and critiquing those who govern is similar to the difference between an NFL quarterback *playing* a game and a coach *watching* the quarterback play the game on film, running it forward and backward, seeing what opportunities were there that he didn't take advantage of at the moment. It's a lot easier for a quarterback to beat an all-out blitz while watching it in slow motion, frame-by-frame, than it is as his offensive line is being overwhelmed and he has two and a half seconds to make the throw.

I'm not degrading the importance of film sessions; they are valuable, and athletes can certainly learn from them. My point is that making the right decisions in real time is much harder than making good decisions after the fact, when we all know what worked and what did not. Decisions look stupid now that may have looked reasonable at the time, and we need to keep that in mind when judging politicians and lawmakers.

This isn't meant to let lawmakers off the hook. In running for office, they assume the responsibilities of office. Politicians shouldn't pursue the job if they don't want to be held accountable. "If you can't stand the heat," Harry Truman famously said, "get out of the kitchen."

What we need are high but realistic expectations for lawmakers. We can't expect anything like perfection; politics is a profession of trial and error, of adjustment and readjustment, of (at times) least bad options. But we *can* reasonably expect from them competence, good judgment, and integrity; basic knowledge about most issues and mastery of a few; the ability to learn from mistakes; and some degree of commitment to the public interest. We should also expect to find, at least now and then, a spirit of sympathy, conciliation, and magnanimity.

In lauding the British style of government compared to the revolutionaries in France, Burke said, "We compensate, we reconcile, we balance. We are enabled to unite into a consistent whole the various anomalies and contending principles that are found in the minds and affairs of men."[38]

The ability to compensate, reconcile, and balance various anomalies and contending principles is not a simple task, and not just anyone off the street can do it. But those we elect to high public office need to.

Which brings me back to the role of citizenship and civic responsibility, to how we think and what we do. In this instance, what we do means getting off the sidelines—refusing to be like spectators.

The qualities that the most active and engaged Americans demand in politicians is what they will get. If enough citizens lend their hands and hearts, their voices and votes to men and women who embody, even if imperfectly, intellectual rigor and wise judgment, mastery of government and moral integrity, our politics will be transformed. But we have to care enough to act. We can't be a nation of onlookers.

The Roman poet Juvenal, writing a century after Jesus was born, satirized the corruption of the Roman citizenry. His most famous indictment of them is that the common people, who previously had not sold their vote to any man, "have abdicated our duties; for the People who once upon a time handed out military command, high civil office, legions—everything, now restrains itself and anxiously hopes for just two things: bread and circuses."[39] By "bread and circuses," he meant the people would be kept happy and docile by a steady diet of trivializing entertainment by those in power. Public support for political leaders ceased to be a result of demanding excellence in public life; it was instead the result of distraction, amusement, circus games. The populace was indifferent to politics, and indifference had a cost.

It still does.

We've stumbled into the "bread and circuses" era in American politics, with the entertainment supplied to us on a daily basis by the president above all but also by others in public office, by social media, and by commentators having frivolous screaming matches on cable news programs. The whole spectacle is dumbing us down. But we are not fated to stay where we are. We can, in the words of the novelist Flannery O'Connor, "push back against the age as hard as it pushes against you."

Politics rightly understood isn't about fun and games, about entertainment and stagecraft. Nor is it merely about expressing one's own values and excoriating the other person's. It's about the hard and intricate work of solving pressing human problems; about getting more big things right than wrong, and in the process making the world a little bit better, a little less inhumane, a little more just.

You and I, our friends and neighbors, our colleagues and acquaintances are the true authors of the American story. We are not like a cork caught in ocean currents, powerless to shape our future. We can shape the outcome of events.

The problems we face as a nation, while significant, are hardly beyond our control or capacity to repair. It is cynical nonsense to assume that what you say and do doesn't matter. The history of America would have been profoundly different if in 1860 it had elected John Breckinridge, Stephen A. Douglas, or John Bell as president instead of Abraham Lincoln.

We're not facing a civil war, a world war, or a great depression.

In fact, as I write these words, America faces no external crisis at all. Instead it faces a crisis of confidence and of comprehension: confidence in the ability of politics to navigate adequately—never perfectly, but adequately—the many conflicts and dilemmas that confront our country; and comprehension of the complexity and compromise that every politician needs to cope with.

True, complaining about politics and politicians is the American way, and it's justified—up to a point. But when it gives way to nihilism, cynicism, and the abdication of governing's hard choices, then it verges on the kind of civic corruption that Juvenal complained of.

As a remedy for nihilism and cynicism, it may be helpful to remember that the politicians who led us through the Civil War, two world wars, and the depression were made of the same flawed human stuff as are the politicians of today. Americans are fortunate that several of them were great, and greatness is certainly in short supply today. But it usually is. And even the great ones made mistakes along the way. In addition, the political systems of their eras, like ours today, struggled with corruption, inefficiency, and disputatiousness.

Politics will never be pretty, but it just needs to work. And for that, it needs a public that will allow it to work.

WHERE DO WE GO FROM HERE?

In June 1966, Senator Robert Kennedy undertook a five-day trip to South Africa during the worst years of apartheid. In the course of the visit, Kennedy met with Nobel Peace Prize winner Chief Albert Lutuli, who had been banned by the government and forced to live in a remote rural area. Kennedy visited Soweto, the largest black township; Stellenbosch, the pro-apartheid Afrikaans university; Johannesburg, the largest city in South Africa; and the University of Cape Town, where he delivered one of his most memorable speeches.

During his address, Kennedy spoke about the need to "recognize the full human equality of all our people before God, before the law, and in the councils of government." He admitted the "wide and tragic gaps" between great ideals and reality, including in America, with our ideals constantly recalling us to our duties. In speaking to young people in particular, he warned about "the danger of futility: the belief there is nothing one man or one woman can do against the enormous array of the world's ills—against misery and ignorance, injustice and violence." Kennedy urged people to have the moral courage to enter the conflict, to fight for their ideals. And using words that would later be engraved on his gravesite at Arlington National Cemetery, he said this:

> Each time a man stands up for an ideal, or acts to improve the lot of others, or strikes out against injustice, he sends forth a tiny ripple of hope, and crossing each other from a million different centers of energy and daring those ripples build a current which can sweep down the mightiest walls of oppression and resistance.[40]

No figure of Kennedy's stature had ever visited South Africa to make the case against institutionalized racial segregation and discrimination. The trip had an electric effect, especially on black South Africans, giving them hope that they were not alone, that the outside world knew and cared about their struggle for equality. One black journalist wrote of Kennedy, "He made us feel, more than ever, that it was still worthwhile, despite our great difficulties, for us to fight for the things that we believed in; that justice, freedom and equality for all men are things we should strive for so that our children should have a better life."[41]

Pressure from both within and outside of South Africa eventually resulted in the end of apartheid, and in 1994 Nelson Mandela, who had been imprisoned at Robben Island during Kennedy's visit because of his antiapartheid efforts, was elected the first black president of South Africa.

America today is not like South Africa in the 1960s. But there is a timelessness to RFK's words, including when he said decisions of government shape all of our lives, and so much that is worthwhile can be swept away when we get things wrong.

Throughout this book I have tried to convey the urgency of the task we face in our time; to argue that because the state of our politics is so poor, and the role politics plays in human flourishing and human suffering is so vital, we need to recover a proper sense of what it is and what it is not.

I have made an effort to explain how we in the United States have ended up in this mess and what we can do to recover from this crisis; how religion can once again elevate our politics and not simply make matters worse. I've shown the power of political rhetoric, how words can build us up or tear us down, and why we need to resist those who, like America's forty-fifth president, are seeking to use words as weapons to annihilate the concept of truth; and I have shown what we can do to support a culture of words and truth, which entails being more loyal to truth than to partisan interests.

This book acknowledges that deep differences will always exist in our country and that the goal of politics is to find ways to live peaceably and even respectfully given those differences. It argues that the democratic virtues of moderation, compromise, and civility are necessary and vital if our society is to function well, and that politics is fundamentally about problem solving. If politics isn't making things better in people's lives, in ways that are concrete and practical, then it's failing in one of its primary responsibilities. I've also tried to show that governing is harder than one might think, and that those who are in the political arena deserve some credit for having entered it.

In writing this book, I've drawn on my personal experiences in politics and government, as well as incidents and lessons from history, with a particular focus on American history. I have brought to this effort my own baggage, imperfections, and limitations. We all see through the glass darkly, seeing things only in part. But I hope I've been able to convey my understanding of the purpose of politics in this book in a way that is accessible and authentic, that is both tough-minded and reasonably fair-minded. I've tried to present an honest account of things. If you find areas of disagreement with me in this book but still believe I've stayed away from caricatures, facile analysis, and simplistic solutions, then count me satisfied.

A few years ago my friend Charles Krauthammer, who passed away last year, published a collection of his writings over the years, *Things That Matter*. It was originally going to be a collection of everything *but* politics. The working title, in fact, was, *There's More to Life Than Politics*. In the end, though, he couldn't do it, for this reason: Charles understood that much lives or dies by politics, and if you get it wrong, everything stands to be swept away. "Politics is the moat, the walls, beyond which lie the barbarians," he wrote. "Fail to keep them at bay, and everything burns."[42]

There are many things that give purpose and meaning to our lives which lie beyond politics—human relationships, family, and friendships; music, movies, and art; sports and philosophy; poetry and books; nature and faith. Our lives are enriched through book clubs and in Bible studies, in volunteering at homeless shelters and at school events, watching our children play sports and act in plays, connecting with old friends, going to NASCAR races and rodeos, visiting art museums and Disney World, hiking in the mountains and taking vacations at the beach. At its best, politics gives us the space to live our lives and pursue our passions—some grand, some ordinary, some silly—and at its very best, politics ennobles us by attaching us to great causes for justice and human dignity.

But that can't happen unless and until we recover a sense of the importance of politics, a respect for the craft of governing and the value of competence and excellence. Sometimes people idealize politics; when they do, it's a mistake. But so is constantly denigrating it. Today we're leaning far too much in the direction of denigration. We need to raise our sights, to expect more from our politicians and from ourselves.

Ours is a remarkable republic, if we can keep it.

ACKNOWLEDGMENTS

No man is an island, entire of itself," John Donne wrote—and the same can be said of a book. That is especially true of a book like this, which was written over the course of a single year, but in important respects is the product of a lifetime in politics.

My journey started at home and in high school, debating my social studies teachers. It included working as an intern in the Washington State senate, at several leading public policy research institutions, as a senior advisor in the White House, and in my current capacity as a contributing writer for the *New York Times* and *The Atlantic*. I have benefited from countless individuals along the way.

In writing this book I owe special thanks to my colleague Yuval Levin. From the conception of this book to its completion, I relied on his insights, wise counsel, and superb editorial suggestions. His contributions were invaluable. Jonathan Rauch was someone I turned to because I knew he would improve the book. He exceeded my expectations in every respect, sharpening the arguments and the language. I owe a great debt of gratitude as well to Michael Gerson, whom I met in the mid-1990s and has been an indispensable source of intellectual, political, and spiritual wisdom. He helped me with this book like he has helped me with practically everything I have written since I have known him.

I am fortunate to have such thoughtful and generous friends.

Speaking of thoughtful and generous friends, David Brooks offered me helpful suggestions early on in the writing of this book. Beyond that, my conversations with David, along with reading his columns, have had a great influence on me.

Kevin Cherry and Donald Harrison offered me helpful insights on individual chapters. Cherie Harder, Will Inboden, and Greg Weiner made suggestions that augmented the book. I'm thankful to each of them.

Philip Yancey read the chapter on faith and politics, and his comments improved it. I'm most grateful to him, though, for how his writing over the years has helped me to understand grace better than I did.

Mickey Maudlin is a superlative editor, wise and discerning. When I pitched the idea for this book to him, he enthusiastically embraced it and then proceeded to help me think it through more carefully. I'm grateful, too, for the outstanding team at HarperOne, including Anna Paustenbach, Courtney Nobile, and Suzanne Quist. My agent, Bob Barnett, is the best in the business. I thank him for his counsel.

When I moved to Washington, DC, in the 1980s, I read one writer with particular intentionality, in hopes of improving myself as a thinker and writer. His name was Charles Krauthammer. Over the years Charles became not only a role model but a close friend. Charles, brilliant and brave, tragically died before this book was published. I miss him deeply. So do millions of others who read his incandescent columns and watched his television commentary.

My editor at the *New York Times*, Aaron Retica, has worked with me on every one of my opinion pieces and made each of them better. In the process he's become a trusted friend. I've only recently begun to work with Yoni Appelbaum, my editor at *The Atlantic*, but it's already clear to me why he's as widely respected as he is.

I want to thank William Bennett, a mentor in my early years in government who among other things taught me the importance and power of ideas in politics. I have many wonderful memories working with him.

Serving President George W. Bush—first as a speechwriter and then as director of the Office of Strategic Initiatives—was the professional honor of a lifetime. The closer I was able to observe him, the more impressed I became with him. He is a man of courage, depth, and decency.

In the course of my years in government, I also had the privilege of working with many colleagues whose lives and work stand as arguments against cynicism about politics. The kind of integrity and commitment to the common good they demonstrated too often goes unmentioned.

One of my first jobs after graduating from college was at the Ethics and Public Policy Center. I left there to work in the Reagan administration and returned two decades later. I am grateful to its president, Ed Whelan, for his support; and for my colleagues, whose collegiality and intellect have made working there a delight.

I also want to extend my thanks to the William and Flora

Hewlett Foundation, and especially to Daniel Stid, for their encouragement, wise counsel, and generous support, without which this book could not have been written; and to the Boisi Family Foundation for its beneficence and faith in my work over the years.

I am a person of the Christian faith, and many people have helped me in my pilgrimage. I want to thank three pastors in particular—Karel Coppock, James Forsyth, and the late Steve Hayner—who have been there when I most needed them. They are the type of people the Apostle Paul had in mind when he referred to "Christ's ambassadors."

I would like to thank the publications that have allowed me to work out in their pages ideas that appear in this book, including *Commentary*, *Christianity Today*, *First Things*, the *New York Times*, *Patheos*, and the Religious News Service. I want to express my gratitude as well to the Miller Center at the University of Virginia, which published an essay I authored included in *Crucible: The President's First Year* (University of Virginia Press); the American Enterprise Institute and its president, Arthur Books, with whom I coauthored *Wealth and Justice: The Morality of Democratic Capitalism*; and the Knight Foundation, which published a White Paper I wrote, "Trust, Facts and the Post-Truth Political Moment."

My greatest debt of gratitude is to those I treasure most—my sons, David and John Paul; my daughter, Christine, who was kind enough to take time away from her Christmas break from college to help me in the endnoting of the book and somehow made it fun; and especially my wife, Cindy. Cindy read the manuscript, made comments and suggestions that improved it, and helped me put finishing touches on it. But above all I am grateful to her for her lovingkindness and for enriching my life in every way imaginable.

I want to thank my sisters, Patti Mushegan and Jackie Olson, and my brother, Al Wehner Jr., for a lifetime of love, laughter, and friendship.

I dedicated this book to my parents, Inge and Alfred Wehner, who gave me life and then blessed it pretty much every day until they passed away. It was Churchill who, in writing to the wife of a friend who died, said, "Great happiness long enjoyed casts its own shadow." My mom and dad cast long shadows. I miss them terribly, but I take comfort in knowing they are in a place where every tear has been wiped away, where the morning has begun, where all things are made new again.

NOTES

Chapter 1: A Noble Calling

1. John Wagner and Scott Clement, "'It's Just Messed Up': Most Think Political Divisions as Bad as Vietnam Era, New Poll Shows," *Washington Post*, October 28, 2017, https://www.washingtonpost.com /politics/its-just-messed-up-most-say-political-divisions-are-as-bad -as-in-vietnam-era-poll-shows/2017/10/27/ad304f1a-b9b6-11e7-9e58 -e6288544af98_story.html?utm_term=.1f85b5f3714e.

Chapter 2: How We Ended Up in This Mess

1. Wagner and Clement, "'It's Just Messed Up.'"
2. Jeffrey M. Jones, "In U.S., Record-Low 47% Extremely Proud to Be Americans," Gallup, July 2, 2018, https://news.gallup.com /poll/236420/record-low-extremely-proud-americans.aspx.
3. Wagner and Clement, "'It's Just Messed Up.'"
4. "Partisanship and Political Animosity in 2016," Pew Research Center, June 22, 2016, http://www.people-press.org/2016/06/22 /partisanship-and-political-animosity-in-2016/.
5. Allstate/Atlantic Media, Heartland Monitor Poll 26, June 19–24, 2016, http://heartlandmonitor.com/wp-content/uploads/2016/07 /Topline_Allstate_Heartland-Monitor-Poll-XXVI_D1client _062816.pdf.
6. Niraj Chokshi, "Trump Voters Driven by Fear of Losing Status, Not Economic Anxiety, Study Finds," *New York Times*, April 24,

2018, https://www.nytimes.com/2018/04/24/us/politics/trump
-economic-anxiety.html.

7. Daniel Cox, Rachel Lienesch, and Robert P. Jones, "Beyond Economics: Fears of Cultural Displacement Pushed the White Working
Class to Trump," PRRI/*The Atlantic*, May 9, 2017, https://www
.prri.org/research/white-working-class-attitudes-economy
-trade-immigration-election-donald-trump/.

8. Sabrina Tavernise, "U.S. Has Highest Share of Foreign-Born Since
1910, with More Coming from Asia," *New York Times*, September 13,
2018, https://www.nytimes.com/2018/09/13/us/census-foreign
-population.html.

9. Kim Parker and Renee Stepler, "As U.S Marriage Rate Hovers at
50%, Education Gap in Marital Status Widens," Pew Research
Center, September 14, 2017, http://www.pewresearch.org/fact
-tank/2017/09/14/as-u-s-marriage-rate-hovers-at-50-education
-gap-in-marital-status-widens/.

10. United States Census Bureau, "The Majority of Children Live with
Two Parents, Census Bureau Reports," November 17, 2016, https://
www.census.gov/newsroom/press-releases/2016/cb16-192.html.

11. Child Trends, "Births to Unmarried Women," September 24, 2018,
https://www.childtrends.org/indicators/births-to-unmarried-women.

12. Bureau of Labor Statistics, "Employment Characteristics of Families Summary," April 19, 2018, https://www.bls.gov/news.release
/famee.nr0.htm.

13. Personal communication, October 23, 2015.

14. For more, see Alan I. Abramowitz, *The Great Alignment: Race,
Party Transformation, and the Rise of Donald Trump* (New Haven,
CT: Yale Univ. Press, 2018).

15. Board of Governors of the Federal Reserve System, "Report on the
Economic Well-Being of U.S. Households in 2017," May 2018,
https://www.federalreserve.gov/publications/files/2017-report
-economic-well-being-us-households-201805.pdf.

16. Justin Fox, "It's Still a Slow-Growth U.S. Economy," Bloomberg,
January 26, 2018, https://www.bloomberg.com/view/articles
/2018-01-26/it-s-still-a-slow-growth-u-s-economy.

17. William Galston, *Anti-Pluralism: The Populist Threat to Liberal Democracy* (New Haven, CT: Yale Univ. Press, 2018), 68.

18. Ronald Brownstein, "Being in the Middle Class Means Worrying About Falling Behind," *The Atlantic*, April 25, 2013, https://www.theatlantic.com/business/archive/2013/04/being-in-the-middle-class-means-worrying-about-falling-behind/426033/.

19. The average student debt is more than $32,000. "Average Student Loan Debt in America: 2019 Facts & Figures," ValuePenguin, https://www.valuepenguin.com/average-student-loan-debt.

20. Arthur C. Brooks and Gail Collins, "What Are We Voting For?," *New York Times*, March 22, 2016, https://www.nytimes.com/2016/03/22/opinion/campaign-stops/what-are-we-voting-for.html.

21. David Leonhardt, "Upward Mobility Has Not Declined, Study Says," *New York Times*, January 23, 2014, https://www.nytimes.com/2014/01/23/business/upward-mobility-has-not-declined-study-says.html?referrer=.

22. Fully 64 percent of Americans believe Congress has made things worse for the middle class, while only 8 percent believe legislators are making things better. Allstate/*National Journal* Heartland Monitor Poll 16, April 5–9, 2013, http://assets.nationaljournal.com/Topline-Results.pdf.

23. Galston, *Anti-Pluralism*, 72.

24. Jonathan Haidt and Sam Abrams, "The Top 10 Reasons American Politics Are So Broken," *Washington Post*, January 7, 2015, https://www.washingtonpost.com/news/wonk/wp/2015/01/07/the-top-10-reasons-american-politics-are-worse-than-ever/?utm_term=.0a2ee0bb9df7.

25. Jonathan Rauch, "How American Politics Went Insane," *The Atlantic*, July/August 2016, https://www.theatlantic.com/magazine/archive/2016/07/how-american-politics-went-insane/485570/.

26. Charles Murray, "The New American Divide," *Wall Street Journal*, January 21, 2012, https://www.wsj.com/articles/SB10001424052970204301404577170733817181646.

27. Lenny Bernstein, "U.S. Life Expectancy Declines Again, a Dismal Trend Not Seen Since World War I," *Washington Post*,

November 29, 2018, https://www.washingtonpost.com/national
/health-science/us-life-expectancy-declines-again-a-dismal-trend
-not-seen-since-world-war-i/2018/11/28/ae58bc8c-f28c-11e8-bc79
-68604ed88993_story.html?utm_term=.6e14da4d781d.

28. Wilfred McClay's preface in Reinhold Niebuhr, *The Children of
Light and the Children of Darkness* (Washington, DC: The Trinity
Forum Reading, 2012), https://www.ttf.org/product/children-of
-light-and-the-children-of-darkness/.

29. Galston, *Anti-Pluralism*, 72.

30. Bryan Burrough, "The Bombings of America That We Forgot,"
Time, September 20, 2016, http://time.com/4501670/bombings-of
-america-burrough/.

31. Kerwin C. Swint, *Mudslingers: The Twenty-Five Dirtiest Political
Campaigns of All Time* (New York: Union Square Press, 2018).

32. Michael Wines, "It Only Seems That Political Corruption Is Rampant," *New York Times*, January 25, 2014, https://www.nytimes
.com/2014/01/26/us/politics/it-only-seems-that-political-corruption
-is-rampant.html.

Chapter 3: What Politics Is

1. Aristotle, *The Politics*, trans. Carnes Lord (Chicago: Univ. of Chicago Press, 1985), 98.

2. Aristotle, *Nicomachean Ethics*, 1099b30, quoted in Edward Clayton,
"Aristotle: Politics," Internet Encyclopedia of Philosophy, http://
www.iep.utm.edu/aris-pol/.

3. Ernest Barker, ed., *The Politics of Aristotle* (Oxford: Oxford Univ.
Press, 1958), li.

4. Clayton, "Aristotle: Politics."

5. Aristotle, *Politics*, 1288b37, quoted in Clayton, "Aristotle: Politics."

6. Carnes Lord, "Editor's Introduction," in Aristotle, *The Politics*, 1.

7. Alan Ryan, *On Politics: A History of Political Thought: From Herodo-
tus to the Present* (New York: Norton, 2012), 1:95.

8. Kenneth Minogue, *Politics: A Very Short Introduction* (Oxford: Oxford Univ. Press, 1995), 10.

9. Ryan, *On Politics*, ch. 13.

10. Frederick Copleston, *A History of Philosophy*, vol. 5 (New York: Doubleday, 1985), 70.

11. It should be noted that Locke's state of nature is quite different from what Hobbes described. For Locke, the state of nature was not synonymous with a state of war. In the former, people can live amicably, at peace and equally, with goodwill toward one another.

12. See John Locke, *Second Treatise of Government*, ed. C. B. Macpherson (Indianapolis: Hackett, 1980), 66.

13. See Locke, *Second Treatise of Government*, xx.

14. "Meeting Minutes of University of Virginia Board of Visitors, 4–5 Mar. 1825, 4 March 1825," *Founders Early Access*, Univ. of Virginia Press, https://rotunda.upress.virginia.edu/founders/default .xqy?keys=FOEA-print-04-02-02-5019.

15. Letter from Thomas Jefferson to John Trumbull, February 15, 1789, Library of Congress, https://www.loc.gov/exhibits/jefferson/18.html.

16. John Locke, "A Letter Concerning Toleration" (1689), Constitution Society, https://www.constitution.org/jl/tolerati.htm.

17. Ryan, *On Politics*, 2:462–63.

18. Lord Charnwood, *Abraham Lincoln* (New York: Henry Holt, 1917), 115.

19. Fred Kaplan, *Lincoln: The Biography of a Writer* (New York: Harper, 2008), 346.

20. William H. Herndon and Jesse William Weik, *The History and Personal Recollections of Abraham Lincoln* (Springfield, IL: Herndon's Lincoln Publishing Company, 1921), 2:414.

21. Stephen B. Oates, *With Malice Toward None: A Life of Abraham Lincoln* (New York: Harper, 1977), 211.

22. William Lee Miller, *President Lincoln: The Duty of a Statesman* (New York: Random House, 2008), 5.

23. Richard Carwardine, *Lincoln: A Life of Purpose and Power* (New York: Vintage, 2007), 50.

24. Carwardine, *Lincoln*, xiii.

25. Allen C. Guelzo, *Lincoln: A Very Short Introduction* (Oxford: Oxford Univ. Press, 2009), 43.

26. Abraham Lincoln, "Address in Independence Hall," February 22, 1861, Abraham Lincoln Online, http://www.abrahamlincoln online.org/lincoln/speeches/philadel.htm.

27. Mario Cuomo and Harold Holzer, eds., *Lincoln on Democracy* (New York: HarperCollins, 1990), 103.

28. Cuomo and Holzer, *Lincoln on Democracy*, 122.

29. For more on this, see Kenneth L. Deutsch and Joseph R. Fornieri, "Introduction," in *Lincoln's American Dream: Clashing Political Perspective* (Dulles, VA: Potomac, 2005).

30. Lord Charmwood, *Abraham Lincoln* (New York: Henry Holt, 1917), 455.

Chapter 4: Politics and Faith

1. John Adams, "From John Adams to Massachusetts Militia, 11 October 1798," Founders Online, https://founders.archives .gov/documents/Adams/99-02-02-3102.

2. A. James Reichley, *Faith in Politics* (Washington, DC: Brookings Institution Press, 200), 94.

3. George Washington, "George Washington on the Importance of Religion to Political Prosperity in His Farewell Speech," Berkley Center for Religion, Peace & World Affairs, Georgetown University, https://berkleycenter.georgetown.edu/quotes/george-washington -on-the-importance-of-religion-to-political-prosperity-in-his -farewell-speech. For a thoughtful discussion of this topic, see the speech by Secretary of Education William J. Bennett, "Religious Belief and the Constitutional Order," University of Missouri, September 17, 1986.

4. C. S. Lewis, *The Abolition of Man* (New York: HarperCollins, 2001), 65.

5. Peter M. Robinson, "Hitchens—The Morals of an Atheist," Uncommon Knowledge, August 23, 2007, http://media.hoover.org /sites/default/files/documents/uk_hitchens_atheist_transcript.pdf.

6. Darryl Hart, *A Secular Faith: Why Christianity Favors the Separation of Church and State* (Chicago: Ivan R. Dee, 2006), 12.

7. Sean A. Adams, "Paul the Roman Citizen: Roman Citizenship in the Ancient World and Its Importance for Understanding Acts 22:22–29," in *Paul: Jew, Greek, and Roman*, ed. Stanley A. Porter (Leiden: Brill, 2009).

8. Personal communication, July 2, 2018.

9. Rabbi Aharon Lichtenstein, "From the Archives (April 27, 1961; Volume 26 Issue 10)—A Consideration of Synthesis from a Torah Point of View," *The Commentator*, January 28, 2018, https://yu commentator.org/2018/01/archives-april-27-1961-volume-26-issue -10-consideration-synthesis-torah-point-view/.

10. Quoted in Martin E. Marty, *A Short History of Christianity* (Minneapolis: Fortress Press, 1987), 40.

11. "Religion in Everyday Life," Pew Research Center, April 12, 2016, http://www.pewforum.org/2016/04/12/religion-in-everyday-life/.

12. Bradford Richardson, "Religious People More Likely to Give to Charity, Study Shows," *Washington Times*, October 30, 2017, https://www.washingtontimes.com/news/2017/oct/30/religious -people-more-likely-give-charity-study/.

13. Simon Vozick-Levinson, "Bono: 'I've Grown Very Fond' of George W. Bush," *Rolling Stone*, November 30, 2018, https://www .rollingstone.com/music/music-news/bono-george-w-bush-world -aids-day-761747/.

14. Martin Luther King Jr., "Letter from Birmingham Jail," April 16, 1963, http://okra.stanford.edu/transcription/document_images /undecided/630416-019.pdf.

15. The troubling trends within the evangelical movement certainly didn't begin with Donald Trump, but they have accelerated since he declared his candidacy in 2015. Moral Majority leader Jerry Falwell Sr., along with Pat Robertson and others, politicized and compromised the evangelical movement in significant ways in the 1980s and 1990s. For more see the book I coauthored with Michael Gerson, *City of Man: Religion and Politics in a New Era* (Chicago: Moody, 2010).

16. Gregory A. Smith, "Churchgoing Republicans, Once Skeptical of Trump, Now Support Him," Pew Research Center, July 21, 2016,

http://www.pewresearch.org/fact-tank/2016/07/21/churchgoing
-republicans-once-skeptical-of-trump-now-support-him/.

17. Sarah Pulliam Bailey, "'Their Dream President': Trump Just
    Gave White Evangelicals a Big Boost," *Washington Post*, May 4,
    2017, https://www.washingtonpost.com/news/acts-of-faith
    /wp/2017/05/04/their-dream-president-trump-just-gave-white
    -evangelicals-a-big-boost/?utm_term=.73bf7923a8af.

18. Jerry Falwell Jr., "Jerry Falwell Jr.: Trump Is the Churchillian
    Leader We Need," *Washington Post*, August 19, 2016, https://
    www.washingtonpost.com/opinions/jerry-falwell-jr-trump
    -is-the-churchillian-leader-we-need/2016/08/19/b1ff79e0
    -64b1-11e6-be4e-23fc4d4d12b4_story.html?utm_term=
    .fe95868251a2.

19. Jessica Taylor, "Trump Nabs Endorsement of a Top Evan-
    gelical Leader," NPR, January 26, 2016, https://www.npr
    .org/2016/01/26/464435834/trump-nabs-endorsement-of-top
    -evangelical-leader.

20. Tweet by Jerry Falwell Jr. (@JerryFalwellJr), January 9, 2018, 7:50 p.m.

21. Quoted in "Focus on the Hypocrisy: Evangelicals Hush Up on
    Trump's Porn Star," *New York Daily News*, January 18, 2018, http://
    www.nydailynews.com/opinion/focus-hypocrisy-evangelicals-hush
    -trump-porn-star-article-1.3765050#.

22. Franklin Graham, "Clinton's Sins Aren't Private," *Wall Street
    Journal*, August 27, 1998, https://www.wsj.com/articles
    /SB904162265981632000.

23. The defenses usually break down into the following categories:
    (a) through history God has done great things through imperfect
    leaders; (b) King David is a hero in the Bible, and he did awful
    things during his life, including committing adultery and engineer-
    ing the murder of the husband of his mistress; and (c) we should
    forgive those who have sinned and fallen short.

24. "Backing Trump, White Evangelicals Flip Flop on Importance of
    Candidate Character: PRRI/Brookings Survey," Public Religion
    Research Institute, October 19, 2016, https://www.prri.org

/research/prri-brookings-oct-19-poll-politics-election-clinton
-double-digit-lead-trump/.

25. Lydia Saad, "Military, Small Business, Police Still Stir Most
    Confidence," Gallup, June 28, 2018, https://news.gallup.com
    /poll/236243/military-small-business-police-stir-confidence
    .aspx?utm_source=twitter&utm_medium=social&utm
    _campaign=military-small-business-police-stir-confidence&utm
    _content=o_social.

26. Timothy Keller, "Can Evangelicalism Survive Donald Trump
    and Roy Moore?," *New Yorker*, December 19, 2017, https://www
    .newyorker.com/news/news-desk/can-evangelicalism-survive
    -donald-trump-and-roy-moore.

27. A superb essay on this subject is Michael Gerson's cover story "The
    Last Temptation" in the April 2018 issue of *The Atlantic*, https://
    www.theatlantic.com/magazine/archive/2018/04/the-last
    -temptation/554066/.

28. C. S. Lewis, *The Screwtape Letters* (New York: HarperCollins,
    2001), 34–35.

29. The idea that America is a hellhole on the verge of moral or eco-
    nomic collapse and that the apocalypse is just around the corner is
    melodramatic and hyperbolic. The United States faces some serious
    problems, of course, as it has at every point in its existence. But
    what goes almost unnoticed these days is that over the last several
    decades several important social indicators—including crime (espe-
    cially violent crime), the divorce rate, and the rate and total number
    of abortions—have declined significantly.

30. "Pastor Robert Jeffress Explains His Support for Trump," *All
    Things Considered*, NPR, October 16, 2016, https://www.npr
    .org/2016/10/16/498171498/pastor-robert-jeffress-explains-his
    -support-for-trump?ft=nprml&f=.

31. Tweet by Jerry Falwell Jr. (@JerryFalwellJr), September 28, 2018,
    8:50 p.m.

32. Edward-Isaac Dovere, "Tony Perkins: Trump Gets 'a Mulligan' on
    Life, Stormy Daniels," *Politico Magazine*, January 23, 2018, https://

www.politico.com/magazine/story/2018/01/23/tony-perkins
-evangelicals-donald-trump-stormy-daniels-216498.

33. Martin Luther King Jr., "A Knock at Midnight," sermon delivered June 5, 1963, recorded June 11, 1967, https://kinginstitute.stanford .edu/king-papers/documents/knock-midnight.

34. Gerson, "Last Temptation."

35. Philip Yancey, *What's So Amazing About Grace?* (Grand Rapids, MI: Zondervan, 1997), 42.

36. New American Standard Bible, Romans 12:2.

Chapter 5: Why Words Matter

1. Alan Brinkley, "The Legacy of John F. Kennedy," *The Atlantic*, Fall 2013, https://www.theatlantic.com/magazine/archive/2013/08/the -legacy-of-john-f-kennedy/309499/.

2. Quote from JFK's 1957 Syracuse University commencement address, where he said, in part, "I would urge therefore that each of you, regardless of your chosen occupation, consider entering the field of politics at some stage in your career. . . . I ask only that you offer to the political arena, and to the critical problems of our society which are decided therein, the benefit of the talents which society has helped to develop in you." Available at John F. Kennedy Presidential Library, https://www.jfklibrary.org/archives/other -resources/john-f-kennedy-speeches/syracuse-university-19570603.

3. Most mornings the director of presidential speechwriting, Michael Gerson, attended the 7:30 a.m. senior staff meeting in the Roosevelt Room. On 9/11, however, I attended in his place. The reason is that Mike was home focusing on a "Communities of Character" speech. We were casting about for a new initiative and rallying point. After the senior staff meeting I wrote Mike an email summarizing the issues we discussed, including a congressional barbeque that was planned for the South Lawn of the White House that evening. My email to Mike began this way: "Very little of note happened." That email was sent five minutes before the first World Trade Center building was hit.

4. Joseph Conrad, *The Nigger of the "Narcissus"* (New York: Norton, 1979), 147.

5. Fred Glueckstein, "'This . . . Is London': Ed Murrow's Churchill Experience an Anglo-American Friendship," *Finest Hour* 144, Autumn 2009, International Churchill Society, https://winstonchurchill.org /publications/finest-hour/finest-hour-144/thisis-london-ed-murrows -churchill-experience-an-anglo-american-friendship/.

6. Jill Lepore, "The Sharpened Quill," *New Yorker*, October 16, 2006, https://www.newyorker.com/magazine/2006/10/16/the-sharpened -quill.

7. J. Gerald Kennedy and Leland S. Person, eds., *The American Novel to 1870*, vol. 5, *The Oxford History of the Novel in English* (New York: Oxford Univ. Press, 2014), 380.

8. David S. Reynolds, *Mightier Than the Sword: Uncle Tom's Cabin and the Battle for America* (New York: Norton, 2011), 90.

9. Reynolds, *Mightier Than the Sword*, 91.

10. Reynolds, *Mightier Than the Sword*, 114.

11. Reynolds, *Mightier Than the Sword*, 114.

12. Reynolds, *Mightier Than the Sword*, 130.

13. Reynolds, *Mightier Than the Sword*, 150.

14. "Donald Trump's Rambling Sentence on July 21, 2015," C-SPAN, March 6, 2017, https://www.c-span.org/video/?c4659595/donald -trumps-rambling-sentence-july-21-2015.

15. Michael Birnbaum and Griff Witte, "Top U.S. Officials Tell the World to Ignore Trump's Tweets," *Washington Post*, February 18, 2018, https://www.washingtonpost.com/world/top-us-officials-tell -the-world-to-ignore-trumps-tweets/2018/02/18/bc605236-14a2 -11e8-942d-16a950029788_story.html?utm_term=.80bb3719443e.

16. Mike Allen and Jonathan Swan, "Trump's Real Plan for 2018," *Axios*, February 12, 2018, https://www.axios.com/trump-plan -2018-culture-war-infrastructure-budget-471751f9-7548-4a8d -9c0e-33f509a4626e.html.

17. Eugene Scott, "President Trump Says NFL Players Who Protest Shouldn't Be in the Game—and Maybe Not Even in the Country," *Washington Post*, May 24, 2018, https://www.washingtonpost.com

/news/the-fix/wp/2018/05/23/president-trump-wanted-consequences
-for-nfl-players-who-protest-racism-before-games-today-he-got
-them/?utm_term=.f77e154d1cff.

18. Eric Bradner, "Conway: Trump White House Offered 'Alternative
Facts' on Crowd Size," CNN, January 23, 2017, http://www.cnn
.com/2017/01/22/politics/kellyanne-conway-alternative-facts/index
.html.

19. Glenn Kessler, Salvador Rizzo, and Meg Kelly, "President Trump
Has Made 9,014 False or Misleading Claims over 773 Days," *Washington Post,* March 4, 2019, https://www.washingtonpost.com
/politics/2019/03/04/president-trump-has-made-false-or-misleading
-claims-over-days/?utm_term=.a98f37cd7a07.

20. Glenn Kessler, "A Year of Unprecedented Deception: Trump Averaged 15 False Claims a Day in 2018," *Washington Post,* December 30,
2018, https://www.washingtonpost.com/politics/2018/12/30
/year-unprecedented-deception-trump-averaged-false-claims
-day/?utm_term=.7e7f004d2ab5.

21. Glenn Kessler, Salvador Rizzo, and Meg Kelly, "President Trump
Has Made 6,420 False or Misleading Claims over 649 Days,"
Washington Post, November 2, 2018, https://www.washingtonpost
.com/politics/2018/11/02/president-trump-has-made-false-or
-misleading-claims-over-days/?utm_term=.213ad1363f8b.

22. Glenn Kessler, Salvador Rizzo, and Meg Kelly, "President Trump
Has Made More Than 5,000 False or Misleading Claims," *Washington Post,* September 13, 2018, https://www.washingtonpost.com
/politics/2018/09/13/president-trump-has-made-more-than-false
-or-misleading-claims/?utm_term=.4094494f1411.

23. Thomas M. Wells, "Donald Trump Hired Me as an Attorney.
Please Don't Support Him for President," *Huffington Post,* July 31,
2016 (updated August 2, 2016), https://www.huffingtonpost.com
/entry/donald-trump-hired-me-as-an-attorneyplease-dont_us_579e
52dee4b00e7e269fb30f?section.

24. Jane Mayer, "Donald Trump's Ghostwriter Tells All," *New Yorker,*
July 25, 2016, https://www.newyorker.com/magazine/2016/07/25
/donald-trumps-ghostwriter-tells-all.

25. Bob Woodward, *Fear: Trump in the White House* (New York: Simon & Schuster, 2018), 357.

26. Woodward, *Fear*, 353.

27. John Wagner, "Anthony Scaramucci: Trump Is Not 'a Liar,' as Previously Said. He's an 'Intentional Liar' Who Uses 'a Methodology of Mistruth,'" *Washington Post*, October 25, 2018, https://www.washingtonpost.com/politics/anthony-scaramucci-trump-is-not-a-liar-as-previously-said-hes-an-intentional-liar-who-uses-a-methodology-of-mistruth/2018/10/25/8dc3fdc4-d879-11e8-a10f-b51546b10756_story.html?utm_term=.7be978d84116.

28. Wagner, "Anthony Scaramucci: Trump Is Not 'a Liar,' as Previously Said. He's an 'Intentional Liar' Who Uses 'a Methodology of Mistruth.'"

29. Just one example of this can be found in an exhaustive *New York Times* report that showed Donald Trump earned his riches through dubious tax schemes and outright fraud. One of the central narratives of his presidential campaign, that he was a successful and wise businessman, was a massive lie. David Barstow, Susanne Craig, and Russ Buettner, "Trump Engaged in Suspect Tax Schemes as He Reaped Riches from His Father," *New York Times*, October 2, 2018, https://www.nytimes.com/interactive/2018/10/02/us/politics/donald-trump-tax-schemes-fred-trump.html.

30. Elizabeth Kolbert, "Why Facts Don't Change Our Minds," *New Yorker*, February 27, 2017, http://www.newyorker.com/magazine/2017/02/27/why-facts-dont-change-our-minds.

31. Jonathan Haidt, *The Righteous Mind: Why Good People Are Divided by Politics and Religion* (New York: Pantheon, 2012), 88.

32. Norbert Schwarz, Eryn J. Newman, and William D. Leach, "Making the Truth Stick and the Myths Fade: Lessons from Cognitive Psychology," *Behavioral Science and Policy* 2, no. 1 (January 2016), https://www.researchgate.net/publication/295478583_Making_The_Truth_Stick_and_The_Myths_Fade_Lessons_from_Cognitive_Psychology.

33. Brian Resnick, "How Politics Breaks Our Brains, and How We Can Put Them Back Together," *The Atlantic*, September 19, 2014,

https://www.theatlantic.com/politics/archive/2014/09/how-politics
-breaks-our-brains-and-how-we-can-put-them-back-together
/453315/.

34. Christine Herman, "Why We Argue Best with Our Mouths Shut,"
Christianity Today, May 26, 2017, http://www.christianitytoday
.com/ct/2017/june/why-we-argue-best-with-our-mouths-shut.html.

35. Herman, "Why We Argue Best with Our Mouths Shut."

36. Margaret Hartmann, "How Australia and Britain Tackled Gun
Violence," *Intelligencer*, October 2, 2015, http://nymag.com/daily
/intelligencer/2015/10/how-australia-and-britain-tackled-gun
-violence.html.

37. "Oxford Dictionaries Word of the Year 2016 Is . . . Post-truth,"
Oxford Dictionaries, November 16, 2016, https://www.oxford
dictionaries.com/press/news/2016/12/11/WOTY-16.

38. "How Journalists Are Rethinking Their Role Under a Trump
Presidency," Diane Rehm, November 30, 2016, http://dianerehm
.org/shows/2016-11-30/how-journalists-are-rethinking-their-role
-under-a-trump-presidency.

39. "Remarks by President Trump at the Veterans of Foreign
Wars of the United States National Convention | Kansas City,
MO," White House, July 24, 2018, https://www.whitehouse
.gov/briefings-statements/remarks-president-trump-veterans
-foreign-wars-united-states-national-convention-kansas-city
-mo/?utm_source=newsletter&utm_medium=email&utm
_campaign=newsletter_axiosam&stream=top-stories.

40. *Meet the Press*, August 19, 2018, NBC News, https://www
.nbcnews.com/meet-the-press/meet-press-august-19-2018
-n901986?utm_source=newsletter&utm_medium=email&utm
_campaign=newsletter_axiosam&stream=top-stories.

41. Aaron Blake, "'Facts Develop': The Trump Team's New 'Alternative
Facts'-esque Ways to Explain Its Falsehoods," *Washington Post*,
August 6, 2018, https://www.washingtonpost.com/news/the-fix/wp
/2018/08/06/facts-develop-the-trump-teams-new-alternative-facts
-esque-ways-to-explain-its-falsehoods/?utm_term=.9a059a8166db.

42. James Poniewozik Tweet (@poniewozik), June 27, 2017, at 6:34 a.m.

43. Jonathan Lemire Tweet (@JonLemire), June 27, 2017, at 12:34 p.m.

44. Lili Loofbourow, "Welcome to Trumplandia, Where Feelings Trump Facts," *The Week*, October 20, 2016, https://theweek.com /articles/656455/welcome-trumplandia-where-feelings-trump-facts.

45. Saad, "Military, Small Business, Police Still Stir Most Confidence."

46. Frank Newport, "Americans' Confidence in Institutions Edges Up," Gallup, June 26, 2017, http://www.gallup.com/poll/212840 /americans-confidence-institutions-edges.aspx?utm_source =twitterbutton&utm_medium=twitter&utm_campaign=sharing.

47. Ian Schwartz, "Full Video: Megyn Kelly Interviews Alex Jones," RealClearPolitics, June 18, 2017, https://www.realclearpolitics .com/video/2017/06/18/full_video_megyn_kelly_interviews_alex _jones.html.

48. Garry Kasparov (@Kasparov63), Twitter, December 13, 2016, 11:08 a.m., https://twitter.com/kasparov63/status/8087505642847 02720?lang=en.

49. For more background on the story, see "About," Issachar Fund, http://www.issacharfund.org/about/.

50. David Roberts, "Donald Trump and the Rise of Tribal Epistemol-ogy," *Vox*, May 19, 2017, https://www.vox.com/policy-and-politics /2017/3/22/14762030/donald-trump-tribal-epistemology.

51. Roberts, "Donald Trump and the Rise of Tribal Epistemology."

52. Carroll Doherty and Jocelyn Kiley, "Key Facts About Partisanship and Political Animosity in America," Pew Research Center, June 22, 2016, http://www.pewresearch.org/fact-tank/2016/06/22/key -facts-partisanship/.

53. Stephen L. Carter, "Torture Report, Rolling Stone and False Di-lemmas," Bloomberg, December 11, 2014, https://www.bloomberg .com/view/articles/2014-12-11/cia-torture-report-rolling-stone -and-false-dilemmas.

54. Michael Barthel and Amy Mitchell, "Americans' Attitudes About the News Media Deeply Divided Along Partisan Lines," Pew Research Center, May 10, 2017, http://www.journalism

.org/2017/05/10/americans-attitudes-about-the-news-media-deeply
-divided-along-partisan-lines/.

55. Derek Thompson, "Report: Journalists Are Miserable, Liberal,
Over-Educated, Under-Paid, Middle-Aged Men—Mostly," *The
Atlantic*, May 8, 2014, https://www.theatlantic.com/business
/archive/2014/05/report-journalists-are-miserable-over-educated
-under-paid-middle-aged-men-mostly/361891/.

56. Margaret Sullivan, "Pro-Trump Media Sets the Agenda with
Lies: Here's How Traditional Media Can Take It Back," *Washington
Post*, March 12, 2017, https://www.washingtonpost.com/lifestyle
/style/pro-trump-media-sets-the-agenda-with-lies-heres-how
-traditional-media-can-take-it-back/2017/03/11/4f30f768-050a
-11e7-b9fa-ed727b644a0b_story.html?utm_term=.c468da1f9027.

57. Maggie Haberman, "Why I Needed to Pull Back from Twitter,"
New York Times, May 20, 2018, https://www.nytimes.com/2018/07/20
/sunday-review/maggie-haberman-twitter-donald-trump.html.

58. Jake Tapper, "LA Press Club Remarks," TapperTumblr, June 26,
2017, http://jaketapper.tumblr.com/post/162277370571/la-press
-club-remarks.

59. "About Us," StopFake.org, http://www.stopfake.org/en/about-us/.

60. Madeleine K. Albright, "We Need 21st Century Responses," Digi-
tal Forensic Research Lab, June 29, 2017, https://medium.com
/@DFRLab/we-need-21st-century-responses-6b7eed6750a4.

61. Hannah Arendt, *Between Past and Future* (New York: Penguin
Books, 1968), 238.

62. Vaclav Havel et al., *The Power of the Powerless* (Armonk, N.Y.:
Palach Press/M.E. Sharpe Inc., 1985), 64–65.

63. George Orwell, *1984* (London: Signet Classics, 1977), 81.

64. Bryan Garsten, *Saving Persuasion: A Defense of Rhetoric and Judgment* (Cambridge, MA: Harvard Univ. Press, 2009), 211–12.

Chapter 6: In Praise of Moderation, Compromise, and Civility

1. James Madison, "The Same Subject Continued: The Union as a
Safeguard Against Domestic Faction and Insurrection: From the

New York Packet, Friday, November 23, 1787," Yale Law School Avalon Project, http://avalon.law.yale.edu/18th_century/fed10.asp.

2. Michael Signer, *Becoming Madison* (New York: PublicAffairs, 2015), 32.

3. That's also true of our propensity to divert controversies to the courts, where those who lose cases feel no sense of democratic fairness. That explains in part why abortion is such a contentious issue nearly a half century after *Roe v. Wade* was decided. The issue was taken out of the hands of the people and turned over to nine justices on the Supreme Court, who issued a sweeping ruling.

4. Greg Weiner, "Nancy Pelosi's First Order of Business Should Be to Reclaim the Power of the House," *New York Times*, November 9, 2018, https://www.nytimes.com/2018/11/09/opinion/sunday /nancy-pelosi-congress-midterms.html?action=click&module= Opinion&pgtype=Homepage.

5. Philip Wallach, "The Indispensable Branch," *National Affairs* 38 (Winter 2018).

6. Personal email, March 8, 2018.

7. Aurelian Craiutu, *Faces of Moderation: The Art of Balance in an Age of Extremes* (Philadelphia: Univ. of Pennsylvania Press, 2017).

8. Alexis de Tocqueville, *Democracy in America*, ed. Phillips Bradley (New York: Vintage Books, 1945), 1:73.

9. Martin Diamond, "The Revolution of Sober Expectations," delivered at Independence Square, Philadelphia, in the House of Representatives Chamber, Congress Hall, October 24, 1973.

10. Harry Clor, *On Moderation: Defending an Ancient Virtue in a Modern World* (Waco, TX: Baylor Univ. Press, 2008), 5.

11. Craiutu, *Faces of Moderation*, ch. 2, 34.

12. Craiutu, *Faces of Moderation*, 148.

13. Amy Gutmann and Dennis Thompson, "The Mindsets of Political Compromise," *Perspectives on Politics* 8 (2010), https://president .upenn.edu/meet-president/mindsets-political-compromise.

14. John F. Kennedy, *Profiles in Courage* (New York: HarperCollins, 2003), 5.

15. Kennedy, *Profiles in Courage*, 5.

16. Jonathan Rauch, "Rescuing Compromise," *National Affairs* 17 (Fall 2013), https://www.nationalaffairs.com/publications/detail /rescuing-compromise.

17. George Washington, "From George Washington to Lafayette, 7 February 1788," Founders Online, https://founders.archives.gov /documents/Washington/04-06-02-0079.

18. James Q. Wilson and John J. DiIulio Jr., *American Government: Institutions and Policies*, 10th ed. (Boston: Houghton Mifflin, 2006), 27.

19. Frederick Douglass, "What to the Slave Is the Fourth of July?," July 5, 1852, TeachingAmericanHistory.org, http://teachingamericanhistory .org/library/document/what-to-the-slave-is-the-fourth-of-july/.

20. Catherine Drinker Bowen, *Miracle at Philadelphia: The Story of the Constitutional Convention May–September 1787* (Boston: Little, Brown and Company, 1966), xii.

21. Weber Shandwick, "Civility in America VII: The State of Civility," June 13, 2017, http://www.webershandwick.com/uploads/news /files/Civility_in_America_the_State_of_Civility.pdf.

22. Stephen L. Carter, *Civility: Manners, Morals, and the Etiquette of Democracy* (New York: Basic Books, 1998), 24.

23. Craiutu, *Faces of Moderation*, 24.

24. Craig Shirley, "In Defense of Incivility," LifeZette, July 30, 2015, https://www.lifezette.com/polizette/in-defense-of-incivility/.

25. Mark Levin, "In Defense of Incivility," PolitBrew, July 30, 2015, http://politibrew.com/politics/2890-mark-levin-in-defense-of -incivility-this-a-great-levin-segment.

26. "William Buckley vs. Gore Vidal" (1968), YouTube, August 15, 2007, https://www.youtube.com/watch?v=nYymnxoQnf8.

27. Andrew Ferguson, "A Buckley Revival," *Weekly Standard*, August 3, 2015, http://www.weeklystandard.com/a-buckley-revival/article /996599.

28. William Lee Miller, *Lincoln's Virtues: An Ethical Biography* (New York: Vintage, 2003), 364.

29. Miller, *Lincoln's Virtues*, 365.

30. John Buchan, *Pilgrim's Way: An Autobiography* (New York: Carroll & Graff Publishers, 1968), 142.

31. C. S. Lewis, *Surprised by Joy: The Shape of My Early Life* (Orlando, FL: Harcourt Brace Modern Classic, 1955), 194.

32. Owen Barfield, *Owen Barfield on C. S. Lewis* (Oxford: Barfield Press, 2011), back cover.

33. Andrew Davison, ed., *Imaginative Apologetics* (London: SCM Press, 2011), 15.

34. George Orwell, *Homage to Catalonia* (Boston: Harcourt, 1952), 230.

35. Philip N. Howard et al., "The IRA, Social Media and Political Polarization in the United States, 2012–2018," Computational Propaganda Research Project, University of Oxford, https://comprop.oii.ox.ac.uk/wp-content/uploads/sites/93/2018/12/IRA-Report-2018.pdf.

36. Sara Fischer, "The Russian Social Media Disease Spread Beyond Facebook and Google," December 18, 2018, https://www.axios.com/russia-interference-facebook-google-social-media-99938baa-5333-4666-bb10-7d796bec7830.html.

37. Robert Pondiscio, "Suing for Civic Education," Thomas B. Fordham Institute, August 1, 2018, https://edexcellence.net/articles/suing-for-civic-education.

38. "How to Teach Civics in School," *The Economist*, July 6, 2017, https://www.economist.com/democracy-in-america/2017/07/06/how-to-teach-civics-in-school.

39. "Americans' Knowledge of the Branches of Government Is Declining," Annenberg Public Policy Center, September 13, 2016, https://www.annenbergpublicpolicycenter.org/americans-knowledge-of-the-branches-of-government-is-declining/.

40. Max Fisher, "Americans vs. Basic Historical Knowledge," *The Atlantic*, June 3, 2010, https://www.theatlantic.com/politics/archive/2010/06/americans-vs-basic-historical-knowledge/340761/.

41. David E. Campbell, Meira Levinson, and Frederick M. Hess, eds., *Making Civics Count: Citizenship Education for a New Generation* (Cambridge, MA: Harvard Education Press, 2012), 1.

42. Leszek Kolakowski, "The Idolatry of Politics" (15th Jefferson Lecture), May 6, 1986, https://neh.dspacedirect.org/handle/11215/3767?show=full.

43. Civics Renewal Network, https://www.civicsrenewalnetwork.org.

44. "The Case for National Service: A Fellowship Research Project for the Panetta Institute for Public Policy," Panetta Institute, http://www.panettainstitute.org/wp-content/uploads/National-Service-Report-Final-as-Published.pdf.

45. William F. Buckley Jr., *Gratitude: Reflections on What We Owe to Our Country* (New York: Random House, 1990), xxi.

46. Buckley, *Gratitude*, 160.

47. "Better Angels Help Communities Ease Political Tensions," *CBS This Morning*, March 26, 2018, available on YouTube, https://www.youtube.com/watch?v=5mLDgtUuK34.

48. "GPS Web Extra: How Americans Can Unify," CNN, https://www.cnn.com/videos/tv/2017/06/17/exp-gps-0618-blankenhorn-web-extra-reconciliation.cnn.

49. Gerald F. Seib, "What Duluth Can Teach America About Declining Political Civility," *Wall Street Journal*, July 30, 2018, https://www.wsj.com/articles/what-duluth-can-teach-america-about-declining-political-civility-1532961081.

50. "Speak Your Peace: The Civility Project @ Duluth Superior Area Community Foundation," Community Foundations, October 20, 2008, available on YouTube, https://www.youtube.com/watch?v=4UpWPDsV-Ww.

51. Duluth Superior Area Community Foundation, "Speak Your Peace: A Civility Project," http://www.dsaspeakyourpeace.org/index.html.

52. Seib, "What Duluth Can Teach America About Declining Political Civility."

53. Yuval Levin, "Going Local in a Troubled Time," *The Catalyst* 11 (Summer 2018), https://www.bushcenter.org/catalyst/your-town/levin-going-local.html.

54. Jamil Zaki, "Kindness Contagion," *Scientific American*, July 26, 2016, https://www.scientificamerican.com/article/kindness-contagion/.

Chapter 7: The Case for Hope

1. An expanded version of the report was published as a book: William J. Bennett, *The Index of Leading Cultural Indicators: Facts and*

Figures on the State of American Society (New York: Simon & Schuster, 1994), 8.

2. Peter Wehner and Yuval Levin, "Crime, Drugs, Welfare—and Other Good News," *Commentary* (December 2007), https://www.commentarymagazine.com/articles/crime-drugs-welfare-and-other-good-news/.

3. The program aired Friday, April 26, 2018.

4. Karoun Demirjian and Josh Dawsey, "Congress Advances Bill to Renew NSA Surveillance Program After Trump Briefly Upstages Key Vote," *Washington Post*, January 11, 2018, https://www.washingtonpost.com/politics/trump-backtracks-after-appearing-to-contradict-his-administrations-support-of-fisa/2018/01/11/5d7f7088-f6d1-11e7-91af-31ac729add94_story.html?utm_term=.fc2c5f77b939.

5. Patrick Radden Keefe, "McMaster and Commander," *New Yorker*, April 30, 2018, https://www.newyorker.com/magazine/2018/04/30/mcmaster-and-commander.

6. Carol E. Lee, Kristen Welker, Stephanie Ruhle, and Dafna Linzer, "Tillerson's Fury at Trump Required an Intervention from Pence," NBC News, October 4, 2017, https://www.nbcnews.com/politics/white-house/tillerson-s-fury-trump-required-intervention-pence-n806451.

7. Carol E. Lee, Courtney Kube, Kristen Welker, and Stephanie Ruhle, "Kelly Thinks He's Saving U.S. from Disaster, Calls Trump 'Idiot,' Say White House Staffers," NBC News, April 30, 2018, https://www.nbcnews.com/politics/white-house/kelly-thinks-he-s-saving-u-s-disaster-calls-trump-n868961.

8. They include the Iraq War and the 2008 financial crisis; the flawed roll-out of the Affordable Care Act/Healthcare.gov website and the poor design of the insurance exchanges; the botched invasion of Libya, which led to the removal from power of Muammar Gaddafi but turned Libya into a terrorist stronghold; the negligence in treatment for veterans by the VA; the Iran-Contra and Clinton-Lewinsky scandals; the Iranian hostage crisis, the energy crisis, and the "stagflation" of the Carter years; the Savings & Loan crisis in the 1980s, which led to what at the time was the most significant

bank collapse since the Great Depression; and the AIDS, crack, and opioid epidemics.

9. "Public Trust in Government Remains Near Historic Lows as Partisan Attitudes Shift," Pew Research Center, May 3, 2017, http://www.people-press.org/2017/05/03/public-trust-in-government -remains-near-historic-lows-as-partisan-attitudes-shift/.

10. Peter H. Schuck, *Why Government Fails So Often: And How It Can Do Better* (Princeton, NJ: Princeton Univ. Press, 2014), 4.

11. Schuck, *Why Government Fails So Often*, 409.

12. Schuck, *Why Government Fails So Often*, 391.

13. Yuval Levin, "Book Review: 'Why Government Fails So Often' by Peter H. Schuck," *Wall Street Journal*, June 9, 2014, https://www .wsj.com/articles/book-review-why-government-fails-so-often-by -peter-h-schuck-1402355950.

14. Aaron Blake, "19 Things Donald Trump Knows Better Than Anyone Else, According to Donald Trump," *Washington Post*, October 4, 2016, https://www.washingtonpost.com/news /the-fix/wp/2016/10/04/17-issues-that-donald-trump-knows -better-than-anyone-else-according-to-donald-trump/?utm _term=.4f72567e1029.

15. William A. Galston, "The Populist Challenge to Liberal Democracy," Brookings, April 17, 2018, https://www.brookings.edu /research/the-populist-challenge-to-liberal-democracy/.

16. Daniele Albertazzi and Duncan McDonnell, eds., *Twenty-First Century Populism* (London: Palgrave Macmillan, 2008), 3.

17. Marshall Frady, *Wallace: The Classic Portrait of Alabama Governor George Wallace* (New York: Random House, 1996), ix, 253.

18. Debbie Elliott, "Is Donald Trump a Modern-Day George Wallace?," NPR, April 22, 2016, https://www.npr.org/2016 /04/22/475172438/donald-trump-and-george-wallace-riding -the-rage.

19. Quoted in Cathleen Decker, "Trump's War Against Elites and Expertise," *Los Angeles Times*, July 27, 2017, http://www.latimes.com /politics/la-na-pol-trump-elites-20170725-story.html.

20. William J. Bennett and John J. DiIulio Jr., "What Good Is Gov-

ernment?," *Commentary* (November 1997), https://www.commentary magazine.com/articles/what-good-is-government/.

21. "The Earned Income Tax Credit," Center on Budget and Policy Priorities, https://www.cbpp.org/sites/default/files/atoms/files /policybasics-eitc.pdf.

22. Hilary W. Hoynes, "Building on the Success of the Earned Income Tax Credit," Brookings, June 19, 2014, https://www.brookings .edu/research/building-on-the-success-of-the-earned-income-tax -credit/.

23. Raymond Aron, *Memoirs: Fifty Years of Political Reflection* (New York: Holmes and Meier Publishers, 1990), 402.

24. Dana Hughes, "Bill Clinton Regrets Rwanda Now (Not So Much in 1994)," ABC News, February 28, 2014, https://abcnews.go.com /Politics/bill-clinton-regrets-rwanda-now-not-so-much-in-1994 /blogEntry?id=22725317.

25. Commission on the Intelligence Capabilities of the United States Regarding Weapons of Mass Destruction, "Report to the President of the United States," March 31, 2005, http://govinfo.library.unt .edu/wmd/report/wmd_report.pdf.

26. "Remarks by the President and First Lady on the End of the War in Iraq," White House, December 14, 2011, https://obamawhite house.archives.gov/the-press-office/2011/12/14/remarks-president -and-first-lady-end-war-iraq.

27. Yuval Levin, *The Great Debate* (New York: Basic Books, 2014), 130.

28. Quoted in Daniel P. Moynihan, "Policy vs. Program in the '70's," *National Affairs* (Summer 1970), https://www.nationalaffairs.com /public_interest/detail/policy-vs-program-in-the-70s.

29. William Greider, "The Education of David Stockman," *The Atlantic*, December 1981, https://www.theatlantic.com/magazine /archive/1981/12/the-education-of-david-stockman/305760/.

30. David Stockman, *The Triumph of Politics* (New York: Harper & Row, 1986), 81.

31. Greider, "The Education of David Stockman."

32. Henry A. Kissinger, *A World Restored*, sentry ed. (Boston, MA: Houghton Mifflin, 1957), 329.

33. Tim Weiner, "Charles W. Colson, Watergate Felon Who Became Evangelical Leader, Dies at 80," *New York Times*, April 21, 2012, https://www.nytimes.com/2012/04/22/us/politics/charles-w -colson-watergate-felon-who-became-evangelical-leader-dies-at -80.html.

34. "Sleazy Backroom Deals on Obamacare," *Washington Examiner*, March 16, 2010, https://www.washingtonexaminer.com/sleazy -backroom-deals-on-obamacare; Brett Norman and Sarah Karlin-Smith, "The One That Got Away: Obamacare and the Drug Industry," *Politico*, July 13, 2016, https://www.politico.com /story/2016/07/obamacare-prescription-drugs-pharma-225444.

35. Moynihan, "Policy vs. Program."

36. George W. Bush, *Decision Points* (New York: Random House, 2010), 333.

37. Bush, *Decision Points*, 334.

38. Edmund Burke, *Reflections on the Revolution in France*, Frank M. Turner, ed. (Binghamton, NY: Yale Univ. Press, 2003), 144.

39. Maryl Gensheimer, *Decorations and Display in Rome's Imperial Thermae* (New York: Oxford Univ. Press, 2018), 242.

40. Robert F. Kennedy, "Day of Affirmation" Speech, June 6, 1966, Cape Town, South Africa, http://www.rfksafilm.org/html/speeches /unicape.php.

41. Juby Mayet, *Golden City Post* (Johannesburg), June 9, 1966; "Background," *RFK in the Land of Apartheid*, http://www.rfksafilm.org /html/back.php.

42. Charles Krauthammer, *Things That Matter* (New York: Random House, 2015), 3.